> Go, and catch a fa...
> Get with child a ...

This plant was believed to ... . insane when it was pulled out of the ground, so dogs were trained to do this instead.

Shakespeare was familiar with the use of drugs for their hypnotic and tranquillising effects. Thus Macbeth:

> Canst thou not minister to a mind diseas'd,
> Pluck from the memory a rooted sorrow,
> Raze out the written troubles of the brain,
> And with some sweet oblivious antidote
> Cleanse the stuff'd bosom of that perilous stuff
> Which weighs upon the heart?

In Hamlet, the King his father is killed by having poison poured into his ear, another route which is not popular with modern drug-takers. In medieval times, and in primitive societies of today, the witch, the witch-doctor and the shaman were feared and courted for their love potions, philtres and aphrodisiacs. The witch could induce the sensation of flying when she rubbed into her skin an ointment containing belladonna (atropine).

The discovery of the Far East and the New World brought to us the benefits of tea (caffeine) and tobacco (nicotine). The symptoms of endemic malaria were controlled by quinine found in cinchona bark from Peru, and in more temperate climates salicylates (aspirin) derived from the willow (*salix*) were found to suppress the ague, rheumatics and fever. South America has grown many plants whose extracts produce exotic and bizarre states of mind conducive to contemplation and mysticism—mescaline from the *peyotyl cactus* of Mexico, psilocybin from *Psilocybe mexicana*, the sacred mushroom, and

Drugs: the Parents' Dilemma

ololinqui from the seeds of the South American Morning Glory. These hallucinogenic substances are the forerunners of modern drugs like lysergic acid diethylamide (LSD).

History repeats itself again and again. Crude extracts are made from a natural plant. This extract is refined and the active principle identified. The effects of this are then intensified by the development of a synthetic analogue; for example—poppy juice, opium, morphine, diacetyl morphine (heroin).

Because man has always wanted to experiment and to control his world and his reactions to it, he has always been a drug-taker. Truly, there is nothing new under the sun.

4

The Classification of Drugs

WE live now in what can be called a drug-taking culture. By that I mean taking drugs is a common aspect of our everyday lives. Look how we advertise them on television, in our magazines and on the sides of our 'buses. Whenever we have a headache, or feel sick or tired, or have eaten indiscriminately, we are exhorted that somewhere there is a tablet that will bring us immediate relief.

Go into your bathroom and look into the cabinet; what do you find? The ubiquitous aspirin and codeine, antiseptics like Dettol or T.C.P., some antibiotics for that bad attack of bronchitis, some sleeping pills, last year's tonic, some cough mixture, perhaps the contraceptive pill, even some anti-depressants forgotten in a corner.

Look in your bedroom and you will find some beauty preparations with hormones to promote the illusions of perpetual youth.

Look in the garage and you will find insecticides and artificial fertilisers.

Look in the living-room and you will find tea, coffee and cocoa, all of which contain caffeine; the cigarettes, cigars and pipe tobacco that contain nicotine; the spirits, wines and beers in the cupboard that contain alcohol.

We are surrounded by drugs in our own homes; we are all drug users, but most of us do not abuse or misuse drugs except on the rare occasion of a party or the evening out.

Drugs: the Parents' Dilemma

Our children are brought up in a world in which they see us, the adults, turn to drugs for relief, comfort and stimulation, and when they grow up it is little surprise that they take to drugs in their turn. What is surprising to them, and considered to be hypocritical, is the indignation of the adult world when youth copies age. There is certainly a problem of drug misuse in young people, but there is equally a problem of drug misuse in older people but it is not talked about and does not hit the headlines because it is not sensational—the middle aged who are dependent on barbiturates to get off to sleep, on appetite suppressants to get their weight down but excite like amphetamines, and on tranquillisers to control the crippling anxiety which would stop them getting through another day.

Drugs are very much a part of modern life; drugs are available, and so drugs are used, and because of human weaknesses, misused.

There are so many drugs we use that we have to classify them into types if we are going to make sense of what is happening. Drugs cannot be lumped together and treated simply as drugs. Each has to be studied in the group from which it comes. Likewise, drug-addicts cannot be condemned together, but each type of addict must be considered for the particular use he makes of his own particular drug. There are various ways we can separate the drugs that are misused.

(a) *Dangerous drugs—non-dangerous drugs:*
This is a bit of a fallacy. All drugs can be dangerous if misused but certainly some are more dangerous than others.

(b) *Hard drugs—soft drugs:*
This implies the same fallacy. Soft drugs like barbiturates, amphetamines, cannabis, LSD are con-

The Classification of Drugs

sidered to be safe, while hard drugs like heroin and cocaine are believed to be dangerous. In fact, soft drugs such as methedrine can be much more dangerous in their effects on the brain and psyche than heroin.

(c) *Opiates—non-opiates:*
This is quite useful. The opiates are a large class on their own and comprise morphine, codeine, pethedine, diacetyl morphine (heroin), and methadone (physeptone). This class has a number of pharmacological properties which set them apart from non-opiates, especially the ease with which physical dependence develops.

(d) *Classification by type of action:*
This is the most comprehensive approach and is a rational way of doing it.

  (i) *Analgesics:*
These kill pain, for example—morphine, heroin, pethedine, codeine and methadone.

  (ii) *Tranquillisers:*
These reduce anxiety and uncomfortable internal emotions, for example—Librium and Valium.

  (iii) *Sedatives:*
In small doses these control tension and agitation, and the same drugs as—

  (iv) *Hypnotics:*
In larger doses induce sleep, for example—alcohol, the barbiturates.

  (v) *Stimulants:*
These act in a way opposite to sedatives and make the brain more active so that the subject feels brighter and wittier, for example—cocaine, amphetamines, methedrine.

(vi) *Hallucinogens:*
These are powerful drugs which in very small doses stimulate the brain and induce marked changes of mood and alter perception, for example—cannabis, mescaline, lysergic acid diethylamide.

These are the different kinds of drugs. I think it helps to keep this simple classification in mind when drugs in general are being discussed. Later, the detailed action of each drug commonly misused will be described more fully.

5

What Causes Addiction?

THE opiates, particularly heroin, when used over a period of time lead to physical and psychological dependence. The basic question always asked is 'why does this happen'?

It is a very complicated subject with many anwers and remains the topic of much research.

The problem has been approached in two ways. Firstly, by looking at what happens to these drugs inside the body and secondly, by looking at what taking the drug does for the addicted person. The first approach has suggested that the drug becomes built into the tissues of the body in such a way that the cells thereafter cannot function properly without it. Cells contain complex chemical factories and the opiate is believed to be absorbed into the chemical reactions in such a way that the opiate becomes an essential component if the chemical reactions are subsequently to occur.

It takes time for this essential dependency to build up. Clinical experience seems to indicate that this dependency may take up to two weeks with a daily dose of about two grains of heroin being taken. This discounts the myth of instantaneous addiction. It used to be thought that one exposure to heroin would lead to inevitable addiction. It takes time to develop, but perhaps in some susceptible subjects, dependence develops more quickly. We just do not yet know enough.

The second approach examines what taking the drug

does for the addicted person. The basic effect is that heroin partially suppresses or inhibits anxiety. We all know how uncomfortable anxiety makes us, and we have experienced the distress of acute anxiety or panic. Heroin suppresses these unpleasant sensations leading to a feeling of placidity and non-involvement. It is like the joke of hitting your head on a brick wall because it is so nice when you stop. The contrast is of itself pleasurable. And then heroin, particularly if injected into a vein, gives the unique feeling which is highly enjoyable. This is called the 'buzz'. Addicts are almost lyrical when they try to describe this effect. They talk of 'liquid fire melting in the stomach' and use terms which suggest the experience is akin to that of sexual intercourse—an explosive excitement followed by a relaxing languor.

This pleasure effect, this buzz, tends to die away in intensity as the addicts become used to the heroin, but it is found that mixing cocaine with heroin (a 'speedball') prolongs the pleasure. And finally, and perhaps most important of all, the addict has to go on taking heroin because if he does not, he experiences highly unpleasant symptoms called withdrawal effects or the abstinence syndrome. Essentially this is a period when the opposite effects of the drug are experienced. There is hyper-arousal and irritability which the addict rushes to neutralise by taking more of the drug. Thus he has to go on taking the drug just to feel comfortable, just to keep withdrawal symptoms at bay. Most heroin addicts find they have to 'fix' every four hours or so just to be comfortable.

Analytical psychology talks of the pleasure–pain principle which states that most human-beings tend to move towards pleasure (a reward) and away from pain (a punishment). Thus an addict will tend to go on taking his drug both for a positive reward of pleasure, but also to avoid the punishment and pain of the withdrawal state.

What Causes Addiction.

Also, behavourial psychology shows that human-beings can be conditioned to behave in a certain way like Pavlov's dogs. A conditioned response which is automatically released, is built up to a certain stimuli. If the response is associated in time with pleasure or gratification, that response tends to be reinforced and repeated in response to the same stimulus next time. In the case of the heroin addict, the stimulus is for him the overwhelming anxiety of a situation and the conditioned response is injecting heroin into a vein.

What is interesting is how powerful these addictive drugs can be in very small doses. For example, it is calculated that a half grain dose of heroin is a four-millionth part of an addict's body weight, and a twenty microgramme dose of lysergic acid diethylamide is a seven-billionth part of body weight, or approximately one molecule of LSD to every three thousand nerve cells in the brain. Such sensitivity is very subtle compared to the grossness of most other human pleasures, such as a pint of beer or three glasses of wine.

Despite all this, other workers have written that dependency is based less on the chemistry of the drug and more on the psychology of the user and the society in which he finds himself.

Personality characteristics and temperament are obviously important. Heroin-takers are often over-driven people with a high internal drive. They have a continual underestimate and poor opinion of themselves. They find it difficult to believe that they can do anything in the long term and must have immediate relief for their anxiety by using the heroin, if they cannot eliminate the source of the anxiety itself. The heroin has both the effect of removing the anxiety and inducing a passive non-involvement in the situation so that the addict feels he is not called upon to do anything about it.

Drugs: the Parents' Dilemma

Avoiding the *withdrawal state* becomes a full-time occupation for the heroin addict. As one young addict is apocryphally said to have declared—as far as he was concerned there was only one drug problem, and that was where to get his next 'fix' from. The horror of the withdrawal state is epitomised in the phrase 'cold turkey'. American addicts put into prison and unable to get any more heroin suffered the distress and dangers of the abstinence syndrome and gave it this nick-name because of one of the effects—a cold clammy skin with pilo-erection or goose pimples.

The whole picture can be divided into five stages:

Stage I (four hours after the last fix): Craving for the drug, anxiety.

Stage II (eight hours): yawning, sweating, running eyes and nose.

Stage III (twelve hours): dilated pupils, goose flesh, muscle twitchings, hot and cold flushes, aching bones and muscles, loss of appetite.

Stage IV (eighteen to twenty-four hours): persistent fever, restlessness, nausea.

Stage V (twenty-four to thirty-six hours): lying curled up on the bed, vomiting, diarrhoea, prostration, sometimes spontaneous sexual orgasms and ejaculations, danger to life and extreme psychological distress.

All these symptoms can be dramatically aborted by a 'fix' of heroin, but if none is available the addict gradually improves as his body makes the painful readjustment of learning to function again without the vital substance. This whole procedure is so distressing that addicts are rarely if ever willing to submit voluntarily to it, and if total withdrawal of heroin is used in hospital treatment the addict is always sedated heavily and the worst effects

What Causes Addiction?

of the abstinence state covered by other psychological drugs.

The drugs which are commonly misused at present fall into six main classes: the barbiturates, the amphetamines, the opiates, cocaine, cannabis, and the hallucinogens. The characteristics of each of these groups is now described in detail, and in a compact form allowing direct comparison. The principle addictive qualities of each of these classes is summarised for convenience in Table One (p. 37). Alcohol and nicotine are added for comparison with the other drugs.

It will be seen that barbiturates, opiates and alcohol fulfil the qualities for physical dependence, that is craving, tolerance and abstinence effects, but that all the drugs produce psychological dependence. Some drugs stimulate consciousness, others depress it and others have both qualities depending on dose and social situation.

BARBITURATES

> We are such stuff
> As dreams are made on, and our little life
> Is rounded with a sleep.
> Shakespeare—*The Tempest*

Historical

The basic substance barbiturate acid so named after its discovery on St. Barbara's day, 1899.

Synthetic derivatives

Amylobarbitone (blue sodium amytal capsules, or white tablets), pentobarbitone (yellow capsules), quinalbarbitone (red capsules), butobarbitone (pink tablets), Tuinal (red and blue capsules), phenobarbitone (white tablets).

Barbiturates are nicknamed 'sleepers' and 'goof balls'.

Drugs: the Parents' Dilemma

Action

Inhibit the grey matter of the brain by depressing glucose metabolism.

Medical use

General anaesthetic given intravenously, night sedatives (hypnotics) or day sedatives in a reduced dose, anticonvulsants.

Taken

Tablets or capsules which are swallowed on their own, or taken in other drinks.

Effects

Produce intoxication like alcohol. Remove inhibition; make the person who takes them drowsy; they show slowed reactions, unsteady gait and slurred speech. The person is drunk without the smell of alcohol on his breath. He shows dilated pupils (compare heroin).

Dependence

Physical and psychological dependence.

Withdrawal

Anxiety, irritability, tremor, insomnia, mental confusion, twitching, convulsions.

Control

Pharmacy and Poisons Act 1933 (Fourth Schedule drugs of the Poisons Rules 1968)—to be sold on prescription only.

Remarks

Not used often by addicts because there is no stimulation and they have a slow action. They are used in

What Causes Addiction?

ADDICTIVE QUALITIES

	CRAVING	TOLERANCE	ABSTINENCE EFFECTS	PSYCHOLOGICAL DEPENDENCE	ALTER CONSCIOUSNESS
BARBITURATES	+	+	+	+	↓
AMPHETAMINES	+	+		+	↑
OPIATES	+	+	+	+	
COCAINE	+			+	↑
CANNABIS				+	↓↑
HALLUCINOGENS				+	↑
ALCOHOL	+	+	+	+	↓↑
NICOTINE	+			+	

+ PRESENT
↓ DEPRESSES
↑ STIMULATES

Drugs: the Parents' Dilemma

combination with other drugs, for example, with amphetamines in the drug Drinamyl. They potentiate the intoxicant effect of alcohol. They are occasionally used in the so-called 'truth-serum' in the form of intravenous Pentothal. It is suggested that some 2 per cent of the population are regularly taking barbiturates at night and it is estimated that some fifty thousand to one hundred thousand persons in the United Kingdom are dependent upon these drugs.

AMPHETAMINES

> Our revels now are ended. These our actors,
> As I foretold you, were all spirits and
> Are melted into air, into thin air:
> (Shakespeare: *The Tempest*)

Historical

These are related to stimulator substances found in the brain and are synthetic derivatives from a naturally occurring substance.

Types

Dexamphetamine (Dexedrine), dextroamphetamine (Durophet), methyl amphetamine (Methedrine), dexamphetamine and amylobarbitone (Drinamyl). These are known as pep pills, sweets, Dexies or Bennies. Some are known as Black Bombers. Drinamyl is now known as French Blues, whereas previously they were known as Purple Hearts. Intravenous methedrine is known as Meths, not to be confused with methylated spirit.

Action

Stimulate the brain cells leading to excitement.

What Causes Addiction?

Medical Use
Mood elevator, the treatment of narcolepsy, appetite suppressant, temporary increase of physical endurance.

Taken
Tablets, capsules, injection (methedrine).

Effects
Nervous excitability, talkativeness, alertness, aggressiveness, dilated pupils, sleeplessness, some increase in sexual feeling. A form of severe mental illness can develop when they are used over a prolonged period or in excess.

Dependence
Psychological dependence but no real physical dependence as such.

Withdrawal
The patient feels uncomfortable; he is lethargic and depressed in mood with a secondary fatigue state. There are no real abstinence syndrome effects as such.

Control
Drugs (Prevention of Misuse) Act 1964—this means unlawful possession.

Remarks
Young people begin to take these to keep awake at all-night parties and for their reputed increase in sexual power. Like alcohol however—'it provoketh the desire, but taketh away the performance.' Leads to the 'Monday morning' syndrome—an inability to wake up after a wild weekend, and recurrent absenteeism at work on Mondays. The original 'Purple Hearts' are now replaced by 'French Blues', so called because they are pale blue in colour and

Drugs: the Parents' Dilemma

are manufactured in France. They are also taken by middle aged bored housewives. The combination with barbiturates allows the worst aspects of each to be built up into an established psychological dependency. Each tends to mask the distressing side effects of the other, and so the drug can be taken in increasing amounts. The number of young people using amphetamines is unknown and likewise the number of middle aged housewives who are dependent upon it. However, there is an estimate that this number may be in the region of one hundred thousand persons.

The Dangers of taking Amphetamines

(a) The elimination of warning signs of fatigue, leading to a psychological and physical collapse.
(b) The possibility of habit formation and psychological dependence.
(c) A severe form of mental illness known as a psychosis, when taken in excess over prolonged periods.
(d) Circulatory effects leading to cardiovascular collapse.

OPIATES

> Thou hast the keys of Paradise, oh just, subtle, and mighty opium!
> (*The Pleasures of Opium:*
> De Quincey, 1856)

Historical

Crude opium derived from the poppy (*Papaver somniferum*). Extract refined—morphine (the sleep bringer). Synthetic derivatives: heroin, pethedine. Other opiates: codeine, methadone (Physeptone). Heroin is known by

What Causes Addiction?

various names such as 'H', 'Stuff', 'Junk' (hence Junkies), 'Horse'.

Action

Kill pain and reduce anxiety, inducing feelings of passivity. Can both stimulate ('buzz') and sedate. Taken in small amounts. One tablet of heroin equals one-sixth of a grain equals ten milligrammes (a 'Jack'). An average dose would be 2 grains (12 tablets) a day.

Medical Use

As pain killers—in injuries, heart thrombosis and in cancer.

Taken

Tablets, linctus, injected under the skin, into a muscle, into a vein (main lining). Occasionally taken in the form of snuff or smoked as a pellet.

Effects

Immediate pleasurable stimulation on injection intravenously ('buzz', 'flash'), thereafter a feeling of well-being or euphoria. Pin-point pupils. Gradual sleepiness. Loss of sexual feeling and cessation of menstruation. Progressive self-neglect in certain cases.

Dependence

Both physical and psychological dependence.

Withdrawal

The abstinence syndrome as previously described.

Control

Dangerous Drugs Acts 1965 and 1967—this means they

Drugs: the Parents' Dilemma

are to be dispensed on prescription only, and heroin addicts in particular require to be notified to the Home Office and supplied with their drug at special clinics.

Remarks

Heroin is the drug of choice for young people who choose to use passive withdrawal from anxiety and conflict, whereas amphetamines seem to be used by more active young people to achieve a dynamic solution. Thomas de Quincey wrote a classic based on his experiences while using opium. In popular literature, the opium dens are the haunt of Chinese dope fiends.

COCAINE

Historical

South American Indians of Bolivia and Peru chewed coca leaves in the mines to give them energy and to dull pain. The alkaloid cocaine was extracted and isolated in 1858. White crystalline powder which glistens like frozen snow, hence the nickname 'snow', also 'C' and 'coke'.

Action

Stimulates the central nervous system when taken orally or intravenously, but it has a local anaesthetic effect when injected into a nerve.

Medical Use

Local anaesthetic in eye-drops, and was used as a local anaesthetic for dental extractions.

Taken

Snuff (erodes the nasal cartilages), injected with heroin ('speedball').

What Causes Addiction?

Effects

It suppresses the inhibitory effect of heroin and prolongs the 'buzz'. In excess, produces hallucinations of small things crawling on or under the skin.

Dependence

Psychological dependence only.

Withdrawal

Usually none.

Control

As for heroin.

Remarks

It is not used on its own, but usually in conjunction with heroin. It may have serious physical effects with prolonged use, because the South American Indians became very emaciated and died prematurely. This of course might be due to other effects in the conditions under which they lived and worked.

CANNABIS

> Herein is not only a great vanity, but a great contempt of God's good gifts, that the sweetness of man's breath, being a good gift of God, should be wilfully corrupted by this stinking smoke.
>
> James IV
> *A Counterblast to Tobacco (1604)*

Historical

Derived from *Cannabis sativa* grown in Southern Asia, Africa and South America. The dried flowering tops are

Drugs: the Parents' Dilemma

made into a smoking mixture and are known as Marihuana, 'Tea', 'Pot'. A resinous extract of cannabis is known as Hashish. This was taken in large amounts by political and religious murderers in the Middle East who were known therefore as 'assassins'. Cannabis has a number of colloquial names depending on how it is taken and how it is used: reefers, grass, weed, ganga tea, pot, etc. The active component of the substance is tetrahydrocannabinol which has hallucinogenic properties.

Action

Effects vary from individual to individual, and in the same person from time to time, and depend very much on his original mood. The drug has both sedative and stimulant properties.

Medical Use

None now, but it was used in a cough sedative as Cannabis Tincture and in certain corn plasters.

Taken

It is usually smoked. The powdered plant or the tincture of cannabis is introduced into a cigarette, known as a reefer.

Effects

It produces an intoxication after some preliminary stimulation. Gradually the subject experiences pleasant sopor in which there is uncontrolled gaiety. There is some distortion of perception. It intensifies the prevailing mood but can induce sudden panics or profound depression.

Dependence

Psychological dependence only.

What Causes Addiction?

Withdrawal

None, except disappointment and resentment when further supplies are not available.

Control

Dangerous Drugs Act 1965—the subject of a controversial debate described later as regards both to the penalties for illegal possession, and the possibility of its use becoming legalised.

Remarks

Those who take cannabis say that they do so because they are curious, to go along with their friends, and because as an intoxicant it is cheaper than alcohol, quicker in effect and has less hangover afterwards. Others who find that they need a drug choose cannabis rather than heroin because they feel that it is on all accounts a much safer drug. When someone is smoking cannabis there is a smell of burning weeds in the room and he looks languid, fatuous and given to ceaseless loud laughter. His face is flushed and his eyes are suffused. It is reported that occasionally a reversible psychosis develops with prolonged and excessive use.

HALLUCINOGENS

Historical

The commonest used drug of this class nowadays is lysergic acid diethylamide (LSD). Ergot fungus grows on the husks of rye, and when this is eaten gives rise to 'St. Anthony's fire' known as ergotisme in France; the subject experiences a burning sensation in the head. The active substance was isolated and was synthesised in 1938 by Sandoz. This is an exceedingly powerful drug in very small quantities. It is known by various names—'acid', 'sugar', 'Zen'.

Action

It is a hallucinogen interfering with the metabolism of powerful brain chemicals producing stimulation and altered perception. Devotees say that it is mind expanding—psychedelic. It reduces the perceptual filter and the user goes on a 'trip'.

Medical Use

It was occasionally used in psychotherapy of a specialised type under close supervision. Recently, work in America suggests that LSD may damage the germinal cells of the sex glands and so it is very rarely, if ever, used now because of this dangerous effect.

Taken

Usually as a drop on a sugar lump, a piece of blotting paper, a biscuit or in a drink.

Effects

There is a delayed period and then the subject experiences distortion of time, space, and colours. Synaesthesia (hearing colours, seeing coloured sounds). There is a regression into the past, and the person feels he is coming out of his body (depersonalisation). Vivid revelatory hallucinations. There are certain dangers in taking LSD, namely a delayed second trip at an inconvenient moment after the first is over; profound depression and panics leading to suicidal behaviour, and the genetical damage as mentioned above.

Dependence

Psychological dependence only.

Withdrawal

None known

Control

Drugs (Prevention of Misuse Act 1964)—illegal possession.

Remarks

This drug has been taken up by intellectuals along with cannabis. Aldous Huxley wrote *The Doors of Perception* (which is called the Old Testament of the Psychedelic movement) and Timothy Leary wrote *Psychedelia* (the New Testament). They serve the new mood for mysticism and the exploration of internal space. Other hallucinogens: mescaline, psilocybin, DMT (dimethyltriptamine), STP (serenity, tranquillity and peace) which is related to the amphetamines.

6

Size and Growth of the Problem

IT is very difficult to determine how many people are using drugs illicitly at any one time. Until there was a system of central notification of drug users, only rough estimates of incidence and prevalence could be made.

As far as barbiturates and amphetamines are concerned the numbers of persons thought to be addicted, estimated at one hundred thousand each, remain approximations only. The extent of cannabis use can, to some extent, be guessed from the number of police prosecutions. In 1966, out of 1,397 drug offences, 1,119 involved cannabis and by 1967, out of 3,024 drug offences, 2,393 were for cannabis. Thus the proportion of cannabis offences has remained reasonably stable at approximately 80 per cent of all the drug offences known to the police, but the absolute number of offences doubled in the year from 1966 to 1967.

Offences figures, of course, only reflect those young people that are caught; many more use cannabis and are never picked up. But how many more remains uncertain at this time.

The Home Office has been collecting figures for those persons known to be dependent on *opiates* from the 1930s onwards, and this gave rise to the idea of registered addicts. These people were compiled on a register but this did not give them the right to obtain drugs as is implied in the term 'registered'. This register was basically a source of information and relied on voluntary notification. It was believed by some authorities that for every one case known to the Home Office there might be another one which was not. In other words the actual number of persons dependent on drugs at any one time might be up to twice that known to the Home Office.

The situation did change in April 1968, because from then on, all addicts receiving heroin and cocaine from recognised treatment centres required to be notified by law. Nevertheless, allowing for the sources of under-reporting, definite patterns and trends in heroin addiction are available and a number of basic facts have emerged. Figure I (p. 50) summarises these facts in graph form.

From the graphs it will be seen that:

(a) From 1947 up to 1959 the number of addicted persons known, remained stable at about 400 cases.
(b) The majority of these were older people who were therapeutic addicts, having the heroin prescribed by doctors for medical reasons, usually intractable pain.
(c) From 1959 onwards there has been a rapidly accelerating increase in the number of known cases.
(d) The increase is made up by an increasing number of young people under the age of thirty-five years who were non-therapeutic addicts. The percentage of young persons under twenty has shown the greatest relative increase thus—the percentage increase for the years 1965 to 1966 in the age group under twenty years was +127 per cent, twenty to thirty-four years was +61 per cent, thirty-five to forty-nine years was +21 per cent and over fifty years

Drugs: the Parents' Dilemma

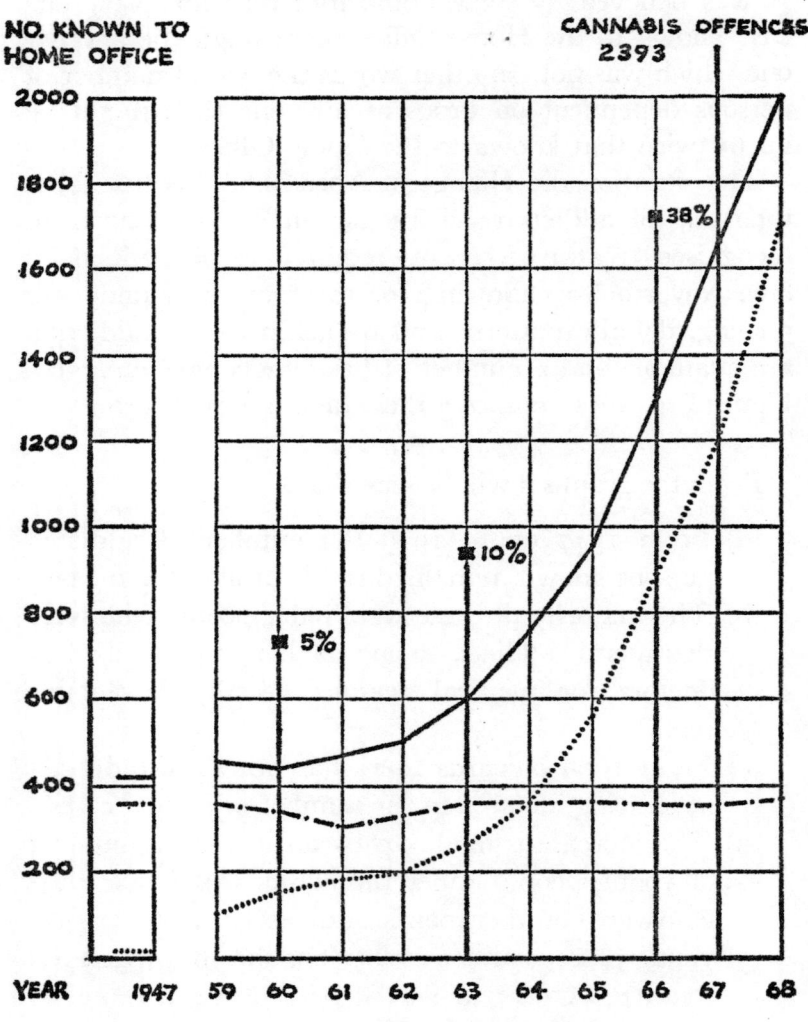

Size and Growth of the Problem

was −2 per cent. This latter decrease in the age group over fifty which is mainly made up of therapeutic addicts, is due to a certain death rate greater than the rate of addiction of newly-addicted persons.

(e) After notification became obligatory in April 1968, the number of addicts known to the Home Office by the end of July 1968 was 1,796.

Dr. Thomas Bewley, a London consultant psychiatrist who has taken a special interest in the study of drug dependent persons, has made an interesting analysis of 1,272 heroin addicts known to the Home Office from 1947 to the end of 1966. This includes the period of rapid expansion of numbers. He shows that there were three males to every one female.

Therapeutic addicts only made up about 3 per cent of the total, and only 13 per cent of the sample were born outside the United Kingdom (these were older men who had been on heroin for more than six years and had come to this country when the Narcotics Regulations were tightened up in their own homelands). 90 per cent of new cases notified each year were under thirty-four and 30 per cent of all new cases notified were under twenty years.

This confirms that the pattern of change in heroin usage has been the increasing number of young people, some of them very young, who are born in this country and are turning to heroin for non-therapeutic purposes.

In the United Kingdom it is estimated now that heroin is used by dependent persons in approximately fifty per million of the population at risk. Alcohol dependence is one hundred times more frequent, but heroin involves the younger more vulnerable sector of the population.

For comparison, in the United States of America the

estimate for heroin use is 280 per million of the population at risk. In the United Kingdom, of the under twenty years age group, the girls first use heroin on average at the age of sixteen and the boys at eighteen. This is another example of the relative advancement of females compared to males.

This means that young people still at school are more likely to be using amphetamines and cannabis than heroin. Heroin taking becomes more likely when they are studying at University or Technical College, or have left school and are in the employment market.

Before heroin was prescribed from special centres it was very expensive to buy on the black market, and so heroin users had to be working or have access to ready cash. Amphetamines, on the other hand, were stolen from chemist shops and were cheaper to buy.

SOURCES OF DRUGS

Given that there has been a rapid increase in the illicit use of drugs, it is interesting to ask where all the drugs come from.

It has to be admitted from the outset that the major source has been the medical profession. Barbiturates are prescribed at the rate of over 16,000,000 scripts per year, and are nearly the commonest prescribed medicine. Supplies are often not used up and left around the home to be picked up by young people. Being unable to sleep is one of the commonest complaints made to doctors who usually respond, even in young patients, with a prescription for a sleeping tablet.

Amphetamines are very popular for reducing weight and large stocks were carried by dispensing chemists. These stocks have frequently been stolen and sold on the black market at a handsome profit. Heroin and cocaine

Size and Growth of the Problem

have nearly always been prescribed by doctors. It is now known that a small group of general practitioners over-prescribed (it is very difficult to be sure just how much drug is really required), and the addicts sold the excess to each other and some 'turned on' other young people who had not had these drugs before. In addition, smaller amounts of heroin and cocaine may have been illicitly imported into the country, to be sold as big business by the commercial 'pushers'.

LSD is not easy to get hold of, but it is rumoured that it is not very difficult to make if you have basic laboratory facilities. It is uncertain how much credence can be given to this.

Cannabis is not used by doctors to any extent, so that most illegal supplies have come from illicitly imported stocks.

What seems to have happened is that a reserve of illicit drugs has been accumulated in the community by various means, and these have been distributed either by pushers as a commercial concern, or by the addicts themselves 'scoring' to their friends, that is selling their own excess. It is known that heroin distribution, for example, involves three people: the person who originally supplies the drug, the addict who is using it and the person he sells to for profit in order to ensure his own future supplies. Once you have a drug-taking sub-culture in the community, this sub-culture ensures that there are ways both of obtaining the drugs, and of distributing them to those who are part of the drug scene. This is at a cost, either in purely monetary terms, or with the implication that 'if I supply *your* need today, I will call on you for *my* need tomorrow'. Addicts do not hand out drugs with gay abandon. If they do share out, it is nearly always for the self-centred reason of ensuring reciprocal supplies later.

Drugs: the Parents' Dilemma

Natural history of drug addiction

In order to find out what happens over time to physically dependent persons, the best thing we can do is to look at what happens to untreated cases. There have not been enough cases to escape professional notice in this country, so we have to turn to the American experience where there have been many more addicts around for a longer time.

Examination of the records of the Federal Bureau of Narcotics shows that about two-thirds of addicts use opiates for a relatively short time, on average for about eight years. These eight years usually occur from the early twenties up to about the age of thirty-five. In these people it seems to be a self-limiting process. In fact, there is a general rule of thumb—the earlier an addict takes to opiates the longer he will use them. This type of research tends to refute the rather frightening belief that many people have, namely, that to go on to heroin is a virtual death sentence.

On the other hand, as research in this country by Dr. Bewley has shown, heroin addicts do have a risk of dying which is some thirty times greater than the risk for those of the same age groups who do not take heroin.

Dr. Bewley has estimated that there is likely to be one death for every thirty-seven persons known to the Home Office per year, which means that there will be approximately forty-eight deaths each year at the present rate of involvement. He has shown the various causes of death to be:

Sudden death (probably due to over-dosage)	29%
Suicide	23%
Sepsis (infection)	22%
'Natural causes'	17%
Violent death	9%

Size and Growth of the Problem

Accidental over-dosage is always possible when the active content of the drug is variable. This is always likely when illegal supplies have been adulterated. These overdoses are associated with sudden collapse due to gross congestion of the lungs. Some of these deaths may be due to a hyper-sensitivity either to the opiate or to to some other contaminating substance. Suicide is always a risk in unstable, impulsive personalities. Sepsis or infection is due to faulty injection techniques and results in jaundice (yellow skin), inflammation of the liver (hepatitis) and very occasionally infections of the heart (endocarditis).

So it seems that if the young addict can get clean supplies together with clean syringes and needles, if he can keep his dose fairly regular and he neither succumbs to suicidal feelings nor is involved in violence, he has a chance as it were of 'growing out of' his physical dependence and maturing to a stage where he can solve his life's problems without resorting to the strategy of drug taking.

7

The Law and Drug Misuse

THE United Kingdom is involved in a number of international agreements to control the distribution of narcotics, in particular the Geneva Convention of 1925 which controlled the manufacture, sale and movement of dangerous drugs such as opiates, cocaine and cannabis. As well as these international agreements there are a number of domestic legal statutes which are designed to control the illegal use of drugs.

The present Dangerous Drugs Acts have been brought into force following the recommendation of the Interdepartmental Committee on Drug Addiction under the chairmanship of Lord Brain, and known as the Brain Committee. This was originally convened in 1958 to advise the Minister of Health and the Secretary of State for Scotland 'on any administrative measures that may seem expedient'.

The Brain Committee published its First Report in 1961 in which it concluded that Drug Addiction should be regarded as an expression of mental disorder rather than as a form of criminal behaviour, and that the problem still seemed to be relatively small for which the current facilities appeared adequate.

Due to the rapid increase in drug use in the early 1960s already described, the Committee was re-convened in July 1964 and it published its Second Report in 1965.

The Law and Drug Misuse

This made a number of observations and recommendations and among those which had the most far-reaching effects were:

(a) The obligatory notification of all persons addicted to dangerous drugs to a central authority.
(b) The setting up of special Treatment Centres, especially in London.
(c) The prescribing of heroin and cocaine should be limited to certain 'licensed' doctors who would operate from special Treatment Centres.

The implications of the Second Report of the Brain Committee are still being worked out in clinical practice and experience.

The legal statutes concerned with drug misuse are:

The Pharmacy and Poisons Act 1933.
The Drugs (Prevention of Misuse) Act 1964.
The Dangerous Drugs Act 1965.
The Dangerous Drugs Act 1967.

(a) *The Pharmacy and Poisons Act 1933*

This lays down the rules for control of poisonous substances and embodies the Poisons Rules 1968 of which the Fourth Schedule lists substances which can be sold by retail, only on the prescription of a duly qualified practitioner. Of these the only group of any importance is the barbiturates. These are not controlled by the Dangerous Drugs Acts and so there is no offence of unlawful possession of barbiturates, only of unlawful supply.

(b) *The Drugs (Prevention of Misuse) Act 1964*

This was first designed to control the misuse of amphetamines and related substances, but subsequently

Drugs: the Parents' Dilemma

the hallucinogens LSD, mescaline, and DMT have been included. The offence under this Act is unlawful possession of the scheduled substances, and the police have powers of arrest against anyone committing this offence, or reasonably suspected of doing so. The offence is an absolute one and it is not necessary to prove that the accused person knew that the thing in his possession was a dangerous drug. The physical existence of the property in his possession is enough.

(c) *The Dangerous Drugs Act 1965*

The Act covers a large area including premises used for smoking or dealing in cannabis, unlawful cultivation of cannabis, and unlawful possession or supply of dangerous drugs. Possession is defined as being 'in his actual custody or is held by some other person subject to his control or for him on his behalf'.

(d) *The Dangerous Drugs Act 1967*

This Act is based on the recommendations of the Second Report of the Brain Committee. On 16 April 1968 the Home Secretary brought out the Dangerous Drugs (Notification of Addicts) Regulations which stipulated that all addicts required thereafter to be notified to the Home Office, and the Dangerous Drugs (Supply to Addicts) Regulations which required only doctors given special permission to do so, to prescribe heroin and cocaine from special treatment centres. Any other doctor who prescribed these drugs to an addicted person was liable to prosecution, but all doctors could still prescribe heroin to those patients whom the doctor considered had an organic illness requiring it.

Intravenous methedrine is now being used more and more by young people, both with heroin and on its own. It is only controlled at present by the Dangerous Drugs

The Law and Drug Misuse

(Prevention of Misuse) Act 1964. Up to very recently, methedrine could still be freely prescribed by any doctor to any patient he wished.

It looks as if intravenous methedrine could become a greater menace than heroin, and it may in the near future have to come under the same kind of stringent safeguards.

At the time of writing this section the Minister of Health has brought out regulations which require methedrine to be available to doctors and dentists, only from a hospital and then only for the doctor's personal use and to be administered by him to the patient in an emergency. This cuts out the prescription of methedrine to drug users.

Another change in the regulations which seems to be imminent at this time is a reduction in the penalties for possessing cannabis. This is a very controversial subject and will be discussed later in the section which goes into the pros and cons of the cannabis debate.

PART 2   The Drug Scene

> Whence are we, and why are we? Of what scene
> The actors or spectators?
> (Shelley—Adonais)

THIS second part of the book is about people involved in the drug scene; about people and the society they live in. It deals with young people and their emotional needs in relationship to each other and to their parents, to the police and to society.

Some young people turn to drugs as one answer to the problems of having to live with others. Parents ask why this happens, could it have been prevented and what can be done about it?

The police act in two roles often believed to be incompatible: on the one hand representing society as the law enforcement agency and on the other, trying to help the young people find a legitimate place in the community.

People have needs and there are various solutions: which they chose is often determined by the social setting and the social climate in which they find themselves.

We, all of us, live in society: the problem is—do we consider ourselves to be involved as actors, or do we merely observe and criticise as spectators?

8

The Needs of Young People

Children sweeten labours; but they make misfortunes more bitter.
(Francis Bacon: *Of Parents and Children*)

ADOLESCENTS, which is what we broadly mean by young people, are a puzzling and disturbing group in our society. Parents give up trying to understand them; it is all too difficult and taxing.

Adolescents in their turn are perplexed to find that the adult world falls far short of the ideal they are seeking as the model on which to base their own lives. There is a generation gap, a credibility gap across which the protagonists argue out and act out their differences. The young people like to think of themselves as unique and in no way owing an allegiance to the past; and the adults look on, perhaps disturbed, more than they are prepared to admit, by the idealism of youth, and guilt tinged with envy can quickly turn to hostility.

Adolescence is an ill-defined period, corresponding roughly to the teen ages, lying between the uncaring world of childhood and the responsibilities of adulthood. It is a bridging period from being dependent on others, to coming of age and having others depend on you. A period of readjustment.

We can talk of *biological adolescence* being that time

when glandular changes occur and secondary sex characteristics emerge. The young person is now capable of reproducing himself. This is the age of awkwardness and self-consciousness as a new body image is built up. *Psychological adolescence* is the time when childish dependency attitudes are gradually replaced by independence, a view of one's own, but this implies knowing who you are, having a sense of personal identity.

You cannot know what you believe in until you know who you are and what you want. One of the commonest emotional disturbances at this time is called an Identity Crisis in which the young person becomes anxious and panic stricken to find he does not know who he is, and he searches feverishly round for a means of establishing an identity. If you take drugs then you know at least that you are a 'drug addict'. You can belong to, identify with, all the other young people who are taking drugs as well as you. And there is a *social adolescence* in which the role of child with all its protection and privileges is being exchanged for the role of adult with its challenges and pains. Home life and school are part of a continuous process of socialisation from infancy, through childhood to adolescence and coming of age.

Many parents and young people are surprised by the intensity of hostility which emerges at this time. Both sides are, as it were, taken by surprise. There is a battle enjoined in which every trick of aggression is used as if 'to the death', which is hardly surprising when we think of it, because this is a struggle for survival; survival in terms of power and authority and freedom to chose for oneself.

Classical analytical theory talks about the *oedipus struggle* and based on the Greek myth in which Oedipus falls unwittingly in love with his own mother Jocasta, and punishes himself for his incestuous guilt. This is a strug-

The Needs of Young People

gle for power and authority in the home: the young man challenges the autonomy of his father, and the young girl rivals her mother in the ways of femininity.

When the parent is challenged in this way the natural reaction is to resent it, and if the challenge is pressed home, to react with aggression and hostility. Meeting resistance in the form of restriction and repression provokes the adolescent to struggle to get 'his parent off his psychic back'. Of course, if you are not very sure of yourself you can fear that you have overdone it and gone too far. You want reassurance that despite all, everything is all right and that the old dependency relationship is still there to fall back on. So the adolescent blows hot and cold, one of the most puzzling and most infuriating characteristics of this age. The parents never know where they stand.

The authority component of parents, typically invested in the father, is projected on to other people in the young person's life who have authority over him—obvious ones like teachers, headmasters, the police, probation officers and such like but less obvious ones like youth leaders, social workers and doctors.

This transference of paternal identification—the 'fatherness' they see in all these persons, means that young people are going to have the same kind of mixed feelings about them, particularly the need to challenge unreasonable authority, by proving that it is wrong.

That is one reason why young people on drugs seem so deliberately to go in the face of all the warnings and advice about the dangers of taking drugs which well-meaning parental figures have given them. There is a perverse need the more they are told a thing is wrong or harmful or dangerous, the more to prove it to themselves that it is not so. This makes any effective educational programme very difficult to provide.

Young people have *emotional needs* as well as physical

ones, and an awareness of these makes their otherwise inexplicable behaviour more comprehensible. These needs can be summarised thus:

(a) *A secure base from which to mature*

A secure base in emotional terms means an explicit assurance of love, of being valued and of being personally accepted. The young person needs to feel that there is a future for him and further, that there is a place for him in that future. Nuclear war and continued fighting in places like Vietnam raise doubts as to whether there is a future and if there is one, whether it is one that the young people want to take part in.

(b) *A need for limits*

Limits imply a structure, a framework of reference in which the adolescent can work out an identity for himself. There must be consistency, fairness and coherent communication. If there are no limits, then rules cannot be defined, and if there are no rules, you run the continuing risk of giving offence to the powers that be. If there are no declared limits adolescents, and adults too for that matter, will test out the situation becoming deliberately provocative in order to force the rules out into the open, and thereby to make the limits evident.

(c) *A need for freedom within these limits*

Limits define the periphery, the extremes of action and reaction. Within these limits the adolescent feels he must have freedom to choose for himself while he explores the contained area and while he experiments, while he finds out for himself. He does not want to accept the truth as dogma from an authority. This requires patience and above all flexibility on the part of those who seek to structure the limits.

(d) A need to contain basic anxiety

Philosophers talk about existential anxiety and mean by this the anxiety which comes from not being certain about oneself and one's standing with one's contemporaries.

The adolescent continually questions himself about his social standing, the adequacy of his sexual functions, his acceptability within his peer group, whether he can compromise with his parents' view or whether he has to reject them outright. He asks who he is and why he is and becomes preoccupied with questions of Being and the meaning of Being. That is why so many go through a religious phase and even take an interest in meditation and mysticism.

(e) A need to cope with crises of confidence

At intervals he loses confidence in himself as a person, in himself in relationship to himself, and at others, in himself as a person in relationship to other persons. This means he will seek for reassurance while at the same time behaving in a way which makes reassurance difficult.

(f) A need to achieve certain goals

He is working towards an independence, a coming of age in the true sense; he is seeking to develop internal controls rather than relying on control imposed from without; he is learning to choose to do or not to do at his own volition; he is searching for an identity, especially in the sexual role, and in a vocational choice.

How does taking drugs help?

The sedative action of drugs controls his excessive and painful anxieties; the stimulant action of drugs induces a feeling of confidence. While he takes drugs he can find an identity, albeit a not very socially acceptable one, in the junkie world, and he can claim an entry into his peer

Drugs: the Parents' Dilemma

group who are taking drugs as well. By using drugs he is testing his parents' and society's limits and making a declaration of independence. Finally, the hallucinogenic drugs aid introspection, the exploration of inner space and leads to a kind of mystical experience.

Of course, drug taking is only one component of adolescent behaviour that parents find puzzling. There is also the unprovoked aggression and hostility, the gang behaviour, the extreme cults, the idealism and rejection of parental standards, often expressed through fashions of clothes and hair styles.

We are at present living through a period of intense adolescent revolt, seen most explicitly in the student unrest. Students, although older than adolescents, share many of their emotional characteristics because at a time when energy is normally being expended in maturing by coming to terms with emotional demands, the students are heavily committed to studying, to gain entry to university or technical college. Once there, the emotional demands which have been temporarily denied can find open expression.

An interesting side-light to this aspect of the struggle is the unprecedented development in which, by education and technological development, young people are truly more knowledgeable in many areas of life than their seniors. For the seniors to claim experience and maturity of judgement, evokes scant respect when these very qualities are synonymous in the student mind with old-fashioned conservatism. The whole drug field is a good example of this—many young people, and students in particular, have taken a great deal of interest in the whole subject, and have read extensively in the literature. They also experiment and speak both from personal experience and informed opinion.

In contrast, many adults have rejected outright drug-

The Needs of Young People

taking by young people and have both condemned it without knowledge, and have made extreme claims which have not been substantiated in fact. Of course, the young people have a vested interest in proving their case, and can be equally guilty of only seeing that side of the argument which substantially agrees with and supports their own position.

Finally, there is a very real way in which teenagers in adolescence have been exploited.

Teenagers have been an important consumer group: they have considerable sums of money to spend on clothes, make-up, pop records, books, and holidays abroad. With the money they have to spend, they have created their own consumer market and allowed their own folk heroes to emerge—not only Che Guevara in the political field, but the Beatles and the Rolling Stones in the world of entertainment. The progression of the Beatles cult from the smoky Cavern Club in Liverpool to the mystical hills of the Himalayas is a good example. In identification with the Teen Scene, these pop idols use drugs and by so doing influence young people in a very subtle way.

Young people are much more ready to listen to their own peer group heroes and martyrs, than to the voice of caution expressed by their parents, by the police and by society at large.

9

The Parents' Dilemma

> The joys of parents are secret, and so are their griefs and fears.
> (Francis Bacon: *Of Parents and Children*)

THE concept of what it means to be a parent is constantly undergoing evolution and change. This does not make it easy to be a parent, especially when aspiring to what is considered to be the ideal of the moment.

The work of child psychologists has made parents more aware of the emotional needs of their children, and this has brought conflicts and fears of failure to the role of parenthood. In earlier days the children were considered to be of less importance than the grown-ups and their care could be delegated to professional child-minders. The Victorian era saw the emergence of the authoritarian parent, to disobey whom brought dire penalties and social ostracism. Then it became important for the parents to be a friend of the children and this often led to them being treated as miniature adults.

The psychological revolution after Freud has emphasised that the growing child has changing emotional needs at each stage of development and that the relationship with the parents must change and grow in parallel. The firmer guidance of the earlier years must give way to increasing opportunities for independence and exploration, but the parent must always be available as a secure emo-

The Parents' Dilemma

tional base for the young person to return to. The ideal parent feels his child's needs and acts in response.

By the time adolescence with all its emotional storms is reached, many parents have given up trying to achieve this ideal. They feel they cannot cope and feel they have somehow failed. The emotional needs of the parents perhaps largely overshadowed until now, begin to express themselves. The child inside the parent, the repressed infantile aspects of adult emotionality, breaks out and demands satisfaction. Envy of youth, coupled with feelings of having failed the adolescent in some way soon turns to irritation, resentment and hostility. The tensions which have always existed between the parent and the child, that have been hidden or ignored, now burst out into the open and cannot be denied.

Each side in the battle resorts to exaggeration of the situation in order to justify its attacks on the other. The initiative towards a reconciliation has to come from the parents who have, after all, fought on both sides of the line, but giving-in, forgiving, and apparently being seen to be defeated are acts which require considerable emotional aplomb and need to be reinforced by some reciprocal act from the other side. Often the emotional temperature is so high, relationships so strained that neither side can give an inch and the battle remains inextricably joined.

Often the only way to escape from too painful conflict is opting out on either side. Young people may opt for their peer group and the solution of drugs; but parents may opt for rejection, and for involvement in matters outside the home. Parents have their own drugs of misuse, of which alcohol is the commonest.

As the role of parent has evolved from the authoritarian, hierarchical Victorian, through the pre-war friendly 'elder brother' attitude to the current attempt to

Drugs: the Parents' Dilemma

face the young as co-equals in status exchanging valid experience, often symbolised by the parents being addressed by their christian names, the aims of parenthood have remained very much the same.

(a) Socialisation

Training the young for life in society; the society within the family and then the society outside in the wider community.

(b) Culturalisation

Perpetuating ideas, feelings and attitudes, the hopes and aspirations, which matter and are vital to the psychological survival of the group.

(c) Protection

Caring for the children when they are young and vulnerable; training them for the day when they must stand on their own and choose for themselves the way they are going to follow.

For the parents of today these aims are getting more and more difficult to follow. For one thing, parents are having their families at an even earlier age. This means that young adults can be faced with the challenges of the adolescence of their children, before they have dealt with the problems of their own. This is a less certain age in which we live: it is not so easy to be sure of the aims of the group to which we belong. There is much greater social mobility and a tendency to blur the outlines of the class boundaries.

Wealth and education which served to set people apart into defined social groups with defined social aims are becoming more equably distributed. It is less easy to know just where you stand and therefore less easy to

The Parents' Dilemma

know what you should stand for. The media of mass communication have increased social awareness and revealed possible alternative standards. There is much to choose from, much to take as your model; the trouble is which to believe, which to adopt as your standards. And always hovering above us all is the idea of the ideal parent that somehow, somewhere, we ought to be striving towards, with the equally present feeling that somehow we are failing, that somewhere we are missing out along the line.

In an age which stresses economic development it is appropriate to talk of parents 'investing' in their children. This can, of course, be quite literal in that parents hope that money spent on the family will bring a rich dividend later, but other parents invest emotion in their children and seek to obtain emotional gratification from them. In a sense these parents can only live emotionally through their children. Every parent is delighted by the successes of the family and distressed by the failures, but there are some parents who unintentionally turn their children into objects, into things; it is then through these objects that the parents are able to be successful, much as chess pieces, inanimate in themselves, moved across the board bring the sweet rewards of victory to the winner.

Most parents want above all their children to be successful. Being happy is also an aim, but it is more nebulous, metaphysical, less easily defined or achieved as being a success. After all, you can work at being a success, whereas happiness comes along as a kind of super-bonus. Being a success in our present culture means:

(a) *Making plenty of money*
(b) *Achieving status in society*
(c) *Being satisfied in a vocation, whether in the realm of employment, or in the realm of home-making.*

Drugs: the Parents' Dilemma

Essentially it means security plus happiness; it also implies wanting what everyone else wants and accepting what everyone else accepts. It means becoming part of the establishment.

For parents the greatest dilemma in bringing up their children is undoubtedly the question of discipline. Discipline cannot be avoided or denied: it is inherent in the process of socialisation, culturalisation and protection. The impulses to immediate self-gratification have to be submitted to the less immediate needs of the group and to long-term gains. Two theoretical approaches are possible —the permissive or the authoritarian.

The *permissive approach* is often thought to be advocated by modern psychologists and enshrined in the injunction 'the child should never be frustrated', with the implications that the child must be allowed to do whatever he wants if he is not to grow up into a neurotic. Modern psychology does not advocate such an approach, but rather asks that the needs of the child, as well as the needs of the parents, should be considered in the family interaction (and the needs of a particular child may be for a declared form of discipline).

The *authoritarian approach* implies both that the parents know best, and also that there will be sanctions if the inviolable right of the parents is challenged. These are extreme theoretical positions; in practice a compromise between the two is what appertains, with a bias towards one or the other. There are times when the young people need a definite stand to react against and thereby to find out what they really want and believe, whereas at others, they need the parents to go along the way with them to let adolescent ideas emerge and be tested out.

The problem is always to know which way to go at a particular time. The best advice is probably to say that the parents should feel what is right for them at that time, and to allow the unconscious recognition of what is the correct course of action to influence their decision.

What might be called the *professional family* has particular difficulties. These are the families where one or other parent has a professional or managerial employment, together with a university standard of education. These families have a number of obvious advantages—a good standard of living, access to the best educational facilities, prestige within our society. But there are also a number of potential disadvantages—there may be a loosening of the marital bond, with husband and wife both having separate lives outside the home; the parents, because of obligations and responsibilities elsewhere, may be less accessible to their children; the care and upbringing of the family may still be delegated to professional child-minders—the school teacher, the youth leader, the baby-sitter, even the child psychologist.

Perhaps what can be most devastating of all is the very success of the parents; the young people have so much to live up to, that they may decide it is impossible, and want to revolt in a kind of protest against what to them is so manifestly unfair.

Also there are difficulties for some parents in asking for help especially from doctors, teachers and the police. They are reluctant to break a family loyalty and to confess a need for help. There is a loss of face, confession of failure to cope—'what would the relatives say, what would the neighbours say if they knew?'—but marshalled against this reluctance there is an awareness that the professionals are a source of help and that they have access to resources which would otherwise be inaccessible to the family. Above all, the professionals do keep confidence. Therefore in needing to ask for help there is *an ambivalence*, a mixture of conflicting feelings. Very often the growing signs of the need overcome the reluctance, but the ambivalence is still there all the same.

Parents should be true to themselves, that is, to allow their own needs to be satisfied, or at least have a chance of being satisfied. Parents need to receive affection as well as give it to the children. They need support from other parents by which to identify in themselves the qualities and role requirements of being a parent and they need support from society, a validation that they are being successful in this task, that they are doing a good job in this area.

Parents need freedom for self-expression as well as looking after the children and the home—they need freedom to be themselves. And above all they need the satisfaction and gratification in feeling a personal sense that they are being successful and moving towards their ego ideal.

The Role of the Police

Superintendent Terence Jones—
Hertfordshire Constabulary

WHY should the law concern itself with an illness? Why should the law enforcers add to their already onerous duties a responsibility for controlling an epidemic?

When there is an outbreak of a disease it is not usually the police who take action. It is the doctors who isolate the germ, contain the epidemic and finally find a cure. But now there is a different epidemic. This time the germs are the very things designed to help medicine—drugs. Drugs, which are provided by nature or invented by man, that make sick people well and well people sick. Now there is a different kind of germ to be isolated, a different problem to contain and a different cure to be sought.

The only way to isolate the drug germ is to ensure that the drugs do not fall into the wrong hands. This means control, licensing, inspection and, if necessary, prosecution. It is here, first of all, where the law must concern itself. And the police, as law enforcement agents, must necessarily become involved.

The control of trafficking in drugs ranges from the uncovering of vast international syndicates making enormous profits, to the teenager passing around pills at a party. Each in their way, is contributing to the increase in the epidemic of drug misuse.

In some ways the indiscriminate trafficking of drugs

Drugs: the Parents' Dilemma

amongst young people is as great a danger as are the big-time drug rings.

No one has any misconceptions about the profit-making pusher. He is a criminal, is generally regarded as such and when he is caught he is usually dealt with accordingly and no one has any regrets. This general condemnation does not always extend to the young person who shares his surplus drugs with his friends but it is just this type of petty trafficking that is responsible for the upsurge of drug abuse in this country during the past few years. If this could be controlled then the problem will be contained.

One of the biggest problems the police encounter when trying to control petty trafficking is that they very rarely see the drugs actually change hands. For obvious reasons, the parties concerned in the exchange generally do so well out of sight of the police. It is because of this that the majority of prosecutions are for being in unlawful possession of drugs. Either the supplier is caught with the drugs before he can pass them on or the recipient is caught after the transaction has been completed. This is one way in which the law hopes to discourage young people swopping drugs, and it is in the process of enforcement that the police necessarily become unpopular with a certain section of society. This unpopularity must, of course, be borne by the police and must not deter them from carrying out this extremely important duty, but it is a factor which makes further work amongst drug users difficult.

An even more complex problem is the relationship between drug taking and crime.

This is not always caused by the actual effect the drug has upon a person. If the potentially violent criminal became a heroin addict it is very doubtful that he would, in fact, become violent. Heroin is a depressant and reduces physical activity. There is no desire on the part of the

The Role of the Police

heroin addict to be violent or even anti-social providing he has his drug. Take away his drug and it is a very different matter. The addict without his heroin is a desperate person indeed and will go to any ends to obtain more. He will lie, cheat, steal and rob because to him heroin is as important as life itself.

Almost opposite is the effect of the stimulants such as amphetamine. Here the normally timid person may suddenly acquire previously unknown bravery and perform anti-social acts. The petty sneak-thief who ordinarily may only dare to break open a gas meter may suddenly feel capable of committing more serious crimes. The passive demonstrator may become militant; the careful driver, a menace.

Other drugs can, of course, cause driving hazards. The person under the influence of cannabis loses his sense of time. Perceptions of space and distance become distorted and he is as much, if not more, a danger as a road user as the person under the influence of alcohol. The same can be said for the drugs which cause hallucinations. Regular use of LSD can cause a 'trip' to recur as long as three or four weeks later. If when this happens the person concerned is driving or working at a machine serious consequences may obviously follow.

Just to what extent drug taking affects the rate of crime is not properly known but it must be accepted that there is a definite connection. In this respect the police have a clear duty to society and it is far from uncommon to see drug dependents before the courts charged with a criminal offence. Here again the police are acting purely in their role as law enforcement agents and although it is to be hoped that society as a whole is behind them, one would hardly expect such actions to foster the affection of the drug dependents.

The terms of reference given to the police are clear.

Drugs: the Parents' Dilemma

High on the list is 'the prevention and detection of crime'. Higher still is 'the protection of life'. This latter concept does not merely confine itself to the lives of the innocent but includes any misguided young person who, with the aid of drugs, embarks on a journey of self-destruction. Justice, then, must be tempered with mercy. Absolute right and absolute wrong must compromise with tolerance and understanding.

Not long after a young person starts taking drugs he begins the process of dropping out of society. 'Turn on, tune in, and drop out' is how they put it themselves.

First of all the drugs are taken secretly without the knowledge of parents or employers. After a while the parents usually notice something different about their child. If amphetamine is the drug of choice the appetite will go as will the desire to sleep. Irritability, hand tremor, perspiration and a dry mouth may all point to abuse of pep pills.

Reluctance to go to work, or the 'Monday morning syndrome', may indicate a weekend of drug taking. A confrontation usually follows.

The next step is greatly dependent upon the relationship between child and parent. Usually, and quite understandably, the first reaction of the parent is horror. Sometimes this gives way to anger, recrimination and an immediate rift. More likely the parents will set about solving the problem themselves. Punitive measures are taken. A curfew is imposed and friends are vetted. Possibly because of the supposed stigma associated with drug taking outside help is not sought. The most important factor is missed. The child is sick.

If he needs drugs he is sick, and the sudden imposition of severe parental control, particularly after a period of permissiveness, will not cure the malady. More likely, in addition to the child's craving for emotional uplift there

The Role of the Police

will also be a feeling of rebellion. The first step towards withdrawal from the family has been taken.

The progression from one drug to another is not necessarily an automatic process but nevertheless it often occurs. Interest in one drug creates interest in the others. The pep pill taker will probably smoke cannabis and vice versa. Some will go further and inject themselves with methedrine, cocaine and heroin. Many will alternate between one drug and another interposing with an occasional dose of LSD. Life becomes totally involved in drugs and the victim becomes part of the 'drug scene'.

Although constantly reassured by their child, who by now has learnt to lie convincingly, the parents will see new changes. Loss of weight; the heroin user's pallor; occasional bouts of retching in the night, blood on clothing and bed linen and then, finally, the first discovery of a syringe. Now horror and resentment are replaced by desolation and despair.

If at this stage parents do not seek help and advice they commit grave neglect. Far better had they consulted the family doctor much earlier. No one would expect parents immediately to inform the police that they suspect their child of taking drugs, but parents seeking advice and information must be assured of a sympathetic reception if they do turn to the police.

The young drug user's work performance will soon begin to suffer. He will drift from job to job and his will to mould a future will soon desert him. He will be more content to join his fellows and sit in a cafe talking and thinking only about drugs. Often by mutual agreement he leaves the family home; stops work altogether and completely 'drops out'. He refuses to comply with the norm and even challenges its correctness. The downhill path has been trodden and it will be a long and laborious climb back.

Drugs: the Parents' Dilemma

The addict will learn a new language. He will be 'blown—or found out, and 'busted'—or arrested. The police will become the 'fuzz'. It will be 'the fuzz' versus 'the scene'. But having reached the twilight world of the drug scene it is often the 'fuzz' who remain the addict's only contact with what used to be.

Many police forces now are training specialised squads of officers to deal specifically with the drug problem. Not only are they trained to recognise drugs and drug takers but they also learn the sociological reasons for drug taking and how best they can persuade or motivate young people to break the habit. In some areas they work closely with the doctors at treatment centres, probation officers, social workers and—most important of all—the parents. Being probably closest of all to the scene these officers learn the language. They learn to communicate with the addicts and, paradoxical as it may seem, the 'fuzz' versus the 'scene' barrier is not so formidable after all.

Addicts are ambivalent. Whilst they are enjoying their drug nothing else in the world matters and life without drugs is unthinkable. But when they are struggling to get fresh supplies and suffering withdrawal effects they long to be free of dependence. They are lonely and unhappy people desperately in need of reassurance. They love to talk about the effects the drugs have on them. Provided one is prepared to listen they will talk for hours and it is astonishing how lucidly and profoundly they can view their drug problems. Perhaps in this way they can form a better appreciation of the plight they are in.

It is when the addict wishes to unburden himself in this way that the trained police officer can help. It is often the policeman who has first contact with the addict and this first contact is crucial. If it is mishandled communication may be lost for ever. The addict is quick to recognise

The Role of the Police

apathy. He will soon know whether the officer knows about drugs.

If the addict realises that he has a better knowledge of the subject than the policeman and can never converse on the same plane he will lose interest. On the other hand, if the addict realises that here is someone who understands about drugs, shows interest in the problem and furthermore displays a willingness to listen and help, it may be that constructive dialogue will follow. If it does, as far as the police are concerned, it is a major breakthrough and in places where it has happened, a great deal of good work has resulted. A tacit understanding grows up. *The addict knows that if he deliberately flouts the law prosecution will be inevitable, but he also knows that if he genuinely seeks help it will be forthcoming.*

It is the contact between addict and policeman that can prove invaluable to those responsible for treatment. Sometimes the addict can be persuaded to attend a treatment centre. Where treatment is carried out mainly on an out-patient basis the police can keep a discreet eye on the patient between attendances. Lapses can sometimes be forestalled and hospital staff can be kept informed of changes in circumstances. Police must not expect reciprocal information from the doctors because, not only must the doctor/patient relationship be respected, but here complete trust is imperative.

Unfortunately facilities for rehabilitation in this country are not yet very abundant and where in-patient treatment is carried out it will probably be for a relatively short period only. On release, unless some special arrangement can be made, the patient is usually permitted to return to the same environment he left only a short time previously. The temptations to relapse are great and here again the police can assist social workers, probation officers and parents in their efforts to reintegrate the patient back into society.

Every policeman's primary task is prevention rather than subsequent detection. This is equally pertinent in the field of drug dependence. Apart from preventing abuse by controlling the illegal distribution of the drugs there is a vast amount of work to be done in giving sensible, factual and constructive advice to the public and increasing their awareness of the problem.

It is a contentious point whether this should extend to police giving advice to school children. One might rightly consider that if education on drugs is to be given to school children it might well be done better by those trained and experienced in teaching. It may also be felt that such a subject should be introduced into the school curriculum rather more imperceptibly and undramatically than by police officers occasionally visiting and giving talks.

An authoritative view is that special lessons on the drugs problem could well prove disastrous and the issue should be woven into the general education course. Here again perhaps the trained police officer can help. Meetings with school teachers and school medical officers help to keep all informed of current trends.

In the long term perhaps enlightened education is the only answer.

Certainly as an immediate measure the acceptance of the fact that there is a problem, albeit affecting as yet only a small minority, is very necessary. No one organisation has a monopoly in the treatment of drug dependence. It can only be a concerted effort by everyone concerned in the welfare of youth that can eventually turn the tide. If we neglect our duty now let us hope that our children or their children, will forgive us.

11

The Society We Live In

> Society everwhere is in conspiracy against
> the manhood of every one of its members
> (R. W. Emerson—*Self Reliance*)

OUR society is characterised by its devotion to science and technology. We are living in an age of expanding technical know-how. The essence of science is enquiry, investigation and experimentation, but there is the danger that science can be elevated to the position of an absolute. The attitude then develops that nothing is of value unless it is scientific or can be submitted to the scrutiny of scientific method.

Technology is the tool of science, but the tool, as the Sorcerer's Apprentice found out, can get out of control and become a tyrant. We can become bemused by the very brilliance of each new discovery—the speed of the computer, the compactness of micro-miniaturised circuits, the power of wonder drugs which combat age-old infections or let us see into the dark crevices of the mind. We have magazines and television programmes dedicated to the promulgation of each new discovery which opens up to us promises of new experience.

There has developed a veritable cult of experience, and as one writer puts it: 'the puritan ethic has been replaced by the hedonistic ethic.' More and more people want to experience, want to know sensation for themselves—young people call it 'living for kicks'. In this kind of culture it is

Drugs: the Parents' Dilemma

inevitable that some will want to explore further for themselves, and the doctrine is preached of the right of the individual to contract out of traditional living, in order to be free to find the brave new world that waits just over the psychological horizon. In America the cult of Psychedelia was born and with it flourish the new religions based on spiritualism and mysticism. We are engaged in a time of intense exploration, exploration both of outer space as we race to the moon and beyond, but also of inner space in the minds of men and women as we race to the heart of feeling and perceiving and being.

Over all this hovers the shadow of the possibility of nuclear war on an immense scale. The splitting of the atom has given man the means of ultimately destroying himself and the question is posed, consciously or unconsciously—have we a future? And if the future is in doubt the immediacy of the present becomes so much more important, and it is vital to squeeze as much as possible from each second of time given to us.

It is vital to maximise impact and contact, and to gain as much time as possible. Sleep can become a threat—perhaps we will miss something as we slumber; being stationary can become a threat—perhaps we are missing something round the next corner. There is anxiety, and the need to stay awake, and the need to move about and the need to maximise use of time and space. Some have found an answer to these needs in drugs—in the sedatives, stimulants and in the hallucinogens.

We are very much a drug conscious society. We demand the right not only to be free from disease, but also to be free from physical and psychological pain. We advertise drugs freely in press and television, we purchase them at will from the chemists, and we ask our doctors to prescribe them in ever-growing amounts. The nation's drug bill in the National Health Service comes to over ten million pounds per year. We use drugs to improve health, to combat infection, to replace what may be missing, to kill pain, to accelerate the healing process, but also to minimise anxiety. The idea of the Lotus-Eaters has charmed men for generations—the idea that somewhere there is that ideal existence free from pain and struggle and effort, and where time is given over solely to the enjoyment of pleasure.

But the Lotus-Eaters never produced anything of lasting value: theirs is a parasitic existence where they take everything and give nothing in return. Anxiety is the spur to ambition, and without it we would be motivated to do nothing. Anxiety is necessary for action, learning and growth. But there can be too much anxiety and over a certain level, the anxiety threshold, performance instead of being enhanced is in fact diminished.

We are looking for something which will reduce unnecessary and excessive anxiety, but in our anxiousness we have gone too far and have asked for anxiety to be removed altogether. The use of drugs in itself is not wrong: it is their use as a means of evasion, as a means to escape from reality and from responsibility that is morally questionable.

Our newspapers and television reflect both what is commercially valuable, but also what fascinates us. We are always being told of the aggression, the violence, the sex with which we are saturated. Deviant behaviour, especially if there is a salacious element, is good 'copy'.

This is all part of living to the full, even if it is for a time only living vicariously through the misdeeds of others. Drug taking fulfils many of these criteria: it is often associated with violence and the criminal world; in the popular mind drugs and sexual behaviour are usually linked together. Drugs are taken to increase sexual performance, or to induce perverted delights or to facilitate deviant practices. Illicit drug use is also forbidden, and

Drugs: the Parents' Dilemma

what is forbidden is, as Adam knows, tinged with a strange attraction.

Drug taking has therefore taken over a large percentage of time and presentation in the media of mass communication. This has popularised it in the original sense of that word, made the people aware of it, if they were not aware of it already. This has helped to make it topical, helped to build it into a fashion and a trend, but a fashion which is persisting because it satisfies needs of the takers, as well as of the onlookers.

Society, like the individuals in it, needs scapegoats. A scapegoat is someone who can be blamed, so as to deflect attention from our own faults. The scapegoat is the object of projected guilt. We laugh at the comedian, or with the comedian, because he makes fun of our scapegoats, makes them an object of ridicule—mothers-in-law, alcoholics, the mentally disturbed, the naive and innocent youth have long been objects of humour, and now it is becoming fashionable to joke about the Junkie and the Pothead. Even a children's programme on television about the Flowerpot Men, one of whose characters is called Weed, has sinister undertones. The young drug taker is a perfect scapegoat; there is the criminal element, the implication of mental instability and the impossibility of youth.

Society needs its scapegoats and is constantly on the look-out for them. With drug taking it has not had to look very far. What is fascinating is that often the scapegoat revels in being one, goes out of his way to behave in such a manner as to incur society's opprobrium. The scapegoat often needs to feel rejected so he in turn can blame society for his failures. He turns to society and says in effect—'you have made me like this'. The drug-taking society can expend its own guilt on the illicit drug user, and he in turn can through this social role give expression to and satisfy his own particular needs.

12

Drugs, Young People and Their Parents

> And sigh that one thing only has been lent
> To youth and age in common—discontent.
> (Matthew Arnold—*Youth's Agitations*)

THE interaction between young people and their parents is characterised by many features, but discontent is shared on both sides.

The need of young people for an ideal on which to build leads to a discontent with adult life with its standards which are seen by youth to be hypocritical and false. Parents, with high hopes for their children, dreaming of success and happiness, feel let down when young people behave in a way which is seen to be a rejection of all that the parents stand for.

Young people are in revolt and this can show itself in a variety of ways, some obvious, some less obvious; revolt can be acted out in ways other than student riots or adolescent vandalism. The best kind of revolt, the most satisfying one is that which is less obvious, that in which parents are unaware that revolt is taking place.

The parents are ignorant of what is happening, and to make a fool of someone is the best way to revolt against them. Open destructiveness and violence are too obvious, and difficult to maintain over a prolonged period. Carefully organised crime is better, but needs effort and

Drugs: the Parents' Dilemma

planning. Direct disobedience is all right only if the parents' wishes are clear and defined. Ignoring parents is possible but something else has to be done in the meanwhile and that takes imagination. Excessive drinking and smoking have been traditional ways of rebellion together with sexual promiscuity, but they are expensive and costly if things go wrong.

Drug taking has offered a perfect way of revolt. It offends so many of society's taboos; it is playing the adults at their own game, but most important of all, side effects —the neutralisation of anxiety or the masking of insecurity, can become an end in themselves. Thus, what might begin as a weapon of revolt, becomes a weapon of self-expression and a weapon of self-preservation. For a vocal minority protest is everything, but for the large numbers that follow on, this secondary gain has become the motivation of the act.

To be young is to want to protest and rebel, to throw out the old and create the new, but for many these ideals get lost in the smoke of marihuana, the visions of LSD and the power of the pep pill. Taking drugs becomes an end in itself, a way of life for a time in which the anxiety and tension of the search for an identity, become too much to bear, too much of an agony only to be escaped from in the fix or the smoke or the trip.

When a parent realises for the first time that a son or a daughter is taking drugs, there is a period of shock and unbelief. 'It can't be true, not our John, not our Mary.' Drug taking, like being killed on the road, is something that happens to *other* people. The numbness is followed by feelings of resentment and rejection and a desire for retribution. The parent is *resentful* that all his love and caring over the years have been thrown in his face. He has given his life to his children and this is how they reward him.

Drugs, Young People and Their Parents

The parent is angry and anger leads to *rejection*. Loving quickly turns to hating, or if not as strong as that, to a wish to have nothing more to do with the person who has caused him this pain. The parent cannot understand why it has happened. He has tried to talk in the past, but he cannot talk now, he feels too choked up about it. Being hurt leads to wanting to hurt back. Someone has done wrong and should be punished for it. *Retribution* carries with it not only the component of revenge, but also the component of restitution—'we can only have him back if he has paid his debt'.

These feelings are not clear-cut but mixed up with one another and also with love for the child and pain in the heart. There is bewilderment—'how could it happen?' and guilt— 'where did we go wrong?' The parent is concerned for the drug taker because he still is a child, but society does not feel these family ties and is not so personally involved. Society's reaction is therefore more primitive and resentment, rejection and desire for retribution more obvious in its ways of dealing with drug takers. Society sees primarily the offence and reacts to this.

These are very strong feelings and very threatening feelings and they can be dealt with in a number of ways.

They can be *denied*: the family can carry on as if nothing has happened; it can refuse to face up to the realities of the situation. The anger and resentment can be *displaced* elsewhere: the family can blame others, blame the authorities for letting it happen, blame the pushers for selling the drugs in the first instance. There can be an *emotional overaction*, a hysteria in which the drug user is made to be the scapegoat for all the family troubles. He is to blame for a nervous breakdown, he has ruined the family's good name, spoiled his sister's chances of a good marriage. And anger can predominate with an *aggressive attack* on the drug user, usually ending up in

Drugs: the Parents' Dilemma

him being thrown out of the home to fend for himself on his meagre resources.

If these first violent counter-reactions can be withstood, the family usually enters into a painful period of mutual readjustment in which each side tries to understand something of the world of the other. At this stage the family finds it cannot cope and turns to others outside itself for help and insight.

People at this time begin asking general questions about why this has happened to our society. Why is there so much use of drugs, especially by young people?

Various answers are given. It is said that use of drugs aids 'drop out'—a way of postponing dealing with problems. Junkies say that they have to work hard at being addicts, and this takes their mind off dealing with their problems of identity and relationship. Others say that use of drugs is an alternative to social revolution. It is felt that there is a need to provide radical alternatives and to change the institutions of society. Young people with their idealism feel this need very much; it seems a gigantic task and no one knows where to begin. So in the meanwhile anxiety can be dulled in dreams and self-awareness cloaked in unreality. It has been argued that the hallucinogens in particular might allow for a greater grasp of ultimate reality which eludes us like a butterfly, but going on a trip really is moving from one illusion into another.

Drugs are used in the artistic world to increase the sensitivity of perception, but no one enduring great work has ever been created under the influence of drugs, although the artist at the time may feel that he has created a masterpiece. Taking hashish allows a mediocre jazz player to live with the illusion that he is one of the greatest.

Drug taking touches on a number of other issues.

What do we mean by the freedom of the individual? Does anyone have the right to choose to behave in such a way that may damage his health, or in the long run increase his chance of dying?

What do we mean by the rights of society? Can society proscribe a form of behaviour which in the general may be harmful, but in the particular may be helpful?

Must the needs of the minority always take second place to the needs of the majority? Has society the right to compel individuals to conform to the admass morality?

The Cannabis Debate exemplifies these issues. Briefly, the advocates wish to free the use of cannabis and leave it to the individual to choose whether he will use it or not, while the opponents claim that there are inherent dangers in the use of the drug and that society must protect its weaker members from their own lack of judgement.

Arguments put up by the *advocates* are as follows:

(*a*) Cannabis is not physically addictive.
(*b*) It is less destructive of personality.
(*c*) It is equivalent in effect to alcohol which is available to those over eighteen years of age.
(*d*) It helps people to feel more creative, and to come to an understanding of themselves.
(*e*) It is a useful, safer alternative to other drugs.
(*f*) It does not automatically lead on to abuse of hard drugs such as heroin.
(*g*) Legal sanctions for its use should be brought into proper perspective. To have the same kind of penalty for using hard drugs implies the dangers are of the same order.
(*h*) While it remains illegal, the black market will prosper with increasing risks of adulterated supplies.

The counter-arguments put up by the *opponents* are:

(*a*) Agreed, but cannabis does cause psychological dependence.

Drugs: the Parents' Dilemma

(b) Agreed, but it is better not to use it at all.
(c) Alcohol has its own dangers, and if it had just become available, it too would probably be more carefully controlled.
(d) This is unproven: people may feel better on it, but may not be better in an objective sense.
(e) It is not a safe drug—psychotic reactions, though rare, do occur, and there is a tendency to gradual deterioration of personal standards with prolonged use.
(f) Agreed, but using cannabis is an entry into a way of life which has its dangers, one of which is the use of hard drugs.
(g) Agreed, and steps are in hand to amend these sanctions.
(h) Agreed, but to prevent a black market is rarely a cogent argument for making a substance freely available.

In addition to these counter-arguments the *opponents* further claim that:

(i) Not enough is known about possible long-term effects in chronic use.
(j) The dose application is uncertain while the drug is smoked and will remain so until the active component—tetrahydrocannabinol is available for prescription.
(k) Doped cigarettes (reefers) are too easily shared around, and there is confusion with the dangers of smoking in general, particularly in young people.

People ask why there is so much drug taking at the present time. This is not an easy question and there are a number of possible answers.

First of all, people have always used drugs as has been

described in Part I; but it has now become fashionable, and is a topic of great interest, and people are concerned about the growing number of very young people involved.

We are going through a period of intense social unrest when all kinds of behaviour are being scrutinised and evaluated—sexual behaviour, relationship between the classes, the value of education—and the use of drugs is part of this social scrutiny. Therefore, we become more aware of it. But there has also been a dramatic increase in drug use in the last ten years and the increase has been greatest in the younger age groups. The *epidemic analogy* is helpful here.

Just as an epidemic of an infectious disease starts from an infected focus and then spreads outwards, by means of cases and carriers, so illicit use of drugs started from a small group of commercial pushers selling the drugs for gain. But there had to be a market for them. This was unwittingly created by a surplus of drugs being available in the community which came from injudicious prescribing by the medical profession.

The drugs were available, young people wanted to experiment and the habit began. In order to get more drugs, users sold some of their excess and so the 'infection' spread outwards. Once the habit was established, the market was there.

Drugs of the barbiturate or amphetamine type are available in homes, or could be stolen from chemists' shops. Forged prescriptions and deceitful practices—for example saying that the drugs were lost or had been spoiled in some way, ensured more supplies and the 'infection' spread further.

Just as with an infectious disease, the contagion spreads with close contact—young people herded together in cafés, dance halls, youth clubs, schools and parties inducted each

Drugs: the Parents' Dilemma

other. If you are 'infected' there is a kind of guilt which can be partly absolved by 'infecting' others.

But to every infection there is built in resistance: innoculation in childhood protects against later small-pox unless infection is overwhelming in virulence; and so with drugs, not all young people are vulnerable, some seem to be protected by influences from childhood. Others not so protected are overwhelmed.

Infection is not inevitable nor necessarily fatal. Some young people take to drugs and then for various reasons give them up and turn to something else. Other young people go on until dependence is established. Again an epidemic continues to expand until it is either contained or a natural immunity develops. In drug taking, measures of containment are being pursued and emotional maturation of those involved in drug use seems to bring a kind of internal immunity.

What Kind of People are likely to become Addicted?

This is a basic question. It used to be thought that there might be a pre-addictive personality, but it is now known that this is not so. It is more helpful to ask why has a given person become addicted, than it is to ask if there are particular groups at special risk. In any one individual there may be a number of motivating factors:

(a) Proselytism plus ignorance

'I like to hand them around' and 'surely if they are manufactured and are available, they must be safe?' Giving things is a way of buying acceptance, and accepting things is a way of forging a relationship.

(b) Group pressures

'I want to belong: they are doing it, so I will do it too.'

The desire to belong to a group as a way of identification and finding oneself, leads to conformity with the drug sub-culture and the drug taking fashion.

(c) *Desire for adventure*

'I am so bored with it all: give me something dangerous every time.' There is a need to give vent to and to satisfy exploratory drives.

(d) *Rebellion against authority*

'I want to do what I think is right. I don't want to be told what I can do and what I can't do. So many of them are so old fashioned it makes me sick.' The need to rebel as a gesture not only of defiance, but also as a declaration of self-autonomy, 'Unless I choose my life for myself, how do I know that I exist or even who I am?'

(e) *Escape from problems*

'You know, everything at times seems too much. Just getting through each day takes an effort. I can't think about the future or what I am going to do. I just want to get by. I'll face the problems later.' Being an addict is a way of life which takes effort and deflects the person from the consideration of his problems, or seems to him to be the only way for the present of coming to some kind of terms with them.

(f) *Dealing with anxiety*

'When I take it, I feel all right. You know, I can get by. It helps me cope with myself. Without it, I get all edgy and restless and nothing is any good any more.' He may be describing the effects of dependence, but these are the very feelings he had before he even started on the drugs. Now he has to go on taking them just to exist from day to day.

* * *

Drugs: the Parents' Dilemma

If these are the kinds of motivations which lead to drug taking, there are still a number of qualities which drug addicts have in common. It is difficult though to be sure if these qualities are what lead to addiction, or whether they are a direct consequence of it.

Various phrases are used by workers to describe addicts: 'unstable character', 'personal inferiority and inadequacy', 'psychologically vulnerable using drugs as a crutch', 'intelligent and sensitive with unsatisfactory emotional relationships in childhood'.

Many of the addicts complain of what might be called 'objectivisation'. An ugly word for an ugly process in which they feel they have been made into a passive object by their parents, as opposed to a person with feelings and wishes and needs. They feel that they have been used somehow by their parents for their own ends, and this has led to them not knowing if they are people in their own right. It has led to them being starved of emotional sensation which they crave through the medium of drugs.

They want to belong, to be valued, to be cherished, to be accepted as themselves. Do addicts value each other in this way?—Yes and no. They care about what of themselves they see in the others. 'If he is hurt in that way, then I can be hurt too, therefore I am concerned for him.' They have an overwhelming sense of rejection and failure in our highly competitive society which puts so much premium on success. They are a kind of second-class citizen who has his own way out through his own value within this chosen sub-culture. At least he can make a success of joining in this group.

In the making of an addict there seem to be three factors:

(a) A pre-disposing inadequacy of personality.

(b) A social and emotional crisis.
(c) A timely offer of a way out through drugs.

Where does the addict get his drugs from?

(a) From a treatment centre or from a general practitioner who is prepared to give them to him.

(b) From the Black Market: from the pool of drugs available in the community, some from illicit import and manufacture, some stolen from chemists, some from over-prescribing.

(c) From his friends, fellow addicts and users, from whom he can borrow a small amount on the understanding that he will help them out later if necessary.

How does he collect his drugs?

Because of a fear of forgery, most addicts never get the actual prescription which is sent direct to a chemist. A certain amount will be prescribed for each day, which has to be collected from that chemist, either all at once or more likely twice or three times in the day. This means that if he is working, he may have to get time off to collect the drugs. If he is unemployed, going round to the chemist becomes a daily ritual and a way of life in itself.

What kind of drugs does he take?

Here there is no set pattern, only trends can be indicated. A number of different drug-using groups can however be identified. First of all, there are those who use pep pills of the *amphetamine* type. They are often taken first to stay awake at a party. The normal clinical dose is one tablet three times a day, but as tolerance develops some young people take up to twenty or thirty at a

Drugs: the Parents' Dilemma

weekend. The record is said to be in the region of fifty tablets over one period.

Barbiturates are taken one or two tablets at a time for a calming effect. Often both of these are taken by the same group.

Cannabis is smoked in the form of a doped cigarette—the reefer and the dose of drug absorbed is very variable. The smoker can go on until he gets a required effect.

LSD is taken in minute doses (microgrammes, one drop on a sugar lump for a given trip). Cannabis and LSD are often taken in a group, because like alcohol the psychological effect is dependent on the social setting and the prevailing mood of the user.

There has been a growing use of *methedrine* taken in an injection into a vein. One ampoule contains thirty milligrammes of the drug and up to three or four ampoules may be injected in a day.

Heroin is also injected in a daily dose of anything from one grain to ten grains. Heroin tablets, each of one-sixth of a grain (a Jack), are dissolved and injected. Heroin users often take in addition *cocaine* in an equivalent dose, or shots of methedrine. Also heroin users take *physeptone* where the effect is dose for dose with heroin.

Where does he take his drugs?

If the addict is on tablets it is quite simple, but if he is injecting himself it is more difficult. He has got to find a quiet place where he can get on with it. Many fix in the chemist's shop if he will allow it. Others make for the nearest public convenience, station waiting room, museum or hospital toilets. They can leave empty phials or blood-stained syringes lying around and this gives rise to offence. Often they are chased away in the middle of a fix and feel, not unreasonably, that they are being hounded.

Drugs, Young People and Their Parents

How does he fix?

Many drug takers carry around tin boxes which contain the syringe and needles, the ampoules or tablets, a candle, teaspoon and matches, and rubber tourniquet. They put on the tourniquet and pump up the vein in the left arm if they are right-handed. They spit on the skin or needle and then plunge in the syringe. This has been charged with the contents of an ampoule or a tablet which has been dissolved in water in the teaspoon heated over the candle (the newer heroin tablets dissolve in cold water). Once in the vein, they suck back some blood to make sure the point of the needle is in place. No one wants to waste a fix by injecting it outside the vein. Then they push the plunger of the syringe home and the fix is completed.

This technique has a number of dangers of which infection is the greatest. The syringe and needle should be new each time. The water used should be sterile and the skin should be swabbed clean with spirit. If syringe and needles are shared, the blood residue can contain a virus which gives rise to serum hepatitis (an infection of the liver) and to jaundice (yellowing of the skin and eyes). Traces of soot can be tattooed into the skin and small abscesses form up the line of the vein. Veins themselves can become blocked due to thrombosis (clotting of the blood). Many of the addicts know of these dangers but do not care: others are very fastidious and take great care of their injecting technique and use clean apparatus. One of the functions of a prescribing centre is to make sure that clean supplies are issued to the addicts.

How often does an addict take his drugs?

This depends on needs and availability. Barbiturates

Drugs: the Parents' Dilemma

and amphetamines are taken when needed, for example at a party or before an interview. Cannabis and LSD are taken usually in a group at a weekend or in the evening when there is time to enjoy the experience. Heroin and cocaine, together with methedrine and physeptone, are taken at regular intervals calculated to keep the withdrawal effects at bay—usually every four hours or so during the waking day with an extra dose before going off to sleep and again on first waking in the morning.

Are there social differences?

There would appear to be certain social groups of drug users. Young people still at school will use amphetamines and occasionally barbiturates. Heroin may be taken occasionally but not regularly. Heroin is (as I observed earlier in this book) usually used after leaving school, largely due to having access and due to the expense. University students and students at technical colleges are likely to use cannabis or LSD, and less likely to use heroin or physeptone. Methedrine is becoming more popular, especially with those of above-average intelligence. People on heroin will also use cocaine and methedrine to counteract the sedative effect of the heroin itself, and they will use physeptone if they can get it, to help out with the heroin when it is rationed or in short supply.

Can an addict work?

Many of them do work and take drugs at the same time, but only if they are not physically incapacitated by the drug and can keep a clear mind during the working day. They also have to be able to collect the supplies on a regular basis if they are taking heroin. Some may be absent on Mondays due to a 'binge' the previous weekend. Others are unable to work because they are too incapacitated by the drugs or because they have lost the will and desire to work. These people are the more severely disturbed psychologically and are taking much larger doses, on a regular and frequent basis.

Many people when they first come across drug taking believe that all the addict wants is an easy life, an excuse not to work and a way to avoid all other social responsibilities. Being an addict is not an easy life—as one young addict said to me, 'Man, you've really got to work hard at it. You're on the go all the time, working towards the next fix and wondering where it's coming from. Treatment centres are all right but you've got to go and get your prescription signed up. Then you've got to pick up your stuff each day from a chemist. You've got to ration yourself, not take it all at once for there is no more where that comes from, unless you are prepared to go out looking for it and there is not much of it around now. Being an addict is not the life for an amateur!'

PART 3   What Can Be Done?

'Brothers, I am sorry I have got no Morrison's Pill for curing the maladies of Society.'
Thomas Carlyle—*Past and Present*.

IN this third part of the book an attempt is made to examine what can be done in the face of problems of illicit drug use. What a parent can do, both to prevent the problem arising, and what he can do thereafter, is first discussed. Parents are members of society, so measures which the community can take, are then described. In any management programme there is a dilemma between being harshly authoritarian on the one hand, and being ineffectively permissive on the other. There is an awareness that any policy of containment involves treating those who are drug dependent in the present, but also of protecting those who might become dependent in the future.

13

Introduction

FACED with a problem of drug misuse, on a personal or on a general basis, most people react after the first emotional impact by asking 'well, what's to be done about it?'

Such an apparently simple question carries within it a number of related questions—'what has been done about it so far?' 'what can be done about it now?' and 'what could be done about it in the future?'

Most of us are used to turning to some authority for the answer when we are faced with such questions. We always assume, rightly or wrongly, that there is someone somewhere who knows the answers. The biggest difficulty is usually finding this omnipotent authority. And so it is with drugs.

People have turned to doctors, to psychologists, to social workers, to teachers and to the police, saying 'Tell us what can be done.' But the one answer which inevitably comes back is 'We don't know; we don't have a ready-made magical answer'. The one thing that we have all learnt is that the problems of drug misuse, for they are many, involve medical, psychiatric, social, educational and cultural factors and that if we are going to find some of the answers, because again there is no one comprehensive answer, we have to approach the difficulties from all these different viewpoints.

People have tried to take one aspect and to isolate it from the others, and by concentrating on it have hoped to find a workable solution. This is what gives rise to essentially meaningless questions such as 'What is the cause of physical dependence?' Whatever may cause physical dependence cannot be isolated from the accompanying emotional and social consequences of being physically addicted.

Some people have tried to deny one or other aspect of the problem as a way of not being involved in it, for example by saying that money should be spent on research into the medical aspects of addiction, advising that addicts should be studied in specially designed centres. I do not mean to imply that such research is not needed but what is dangerous I think is the implication that such research can be done in isolation and independently from other lines of enquiry.

Drug misuse is a social phenomenon with medical, psychological, cultural, educational and penal aspects, and can only be approached in this comprehensive way. The comprehensive approach means a team approach, and there must be co-operation and co-ordination within the team, and above all there must be communication between the various constituent members of the team that is trying to help.

It is interesting to note in passing that there is an unusual aspect to this particular social problem, and that is that those requiring or seeking help know more about the problem than the professionals who are asked to help. There is also the uncomfortable situation that they too seem to be more effective than the professionals when it comes to giving help.

Doctor Ramirez, New York's Commissioner of the Addiction Services Agency, has shown that the most potent helper in the team dealing with addicted people is the addict himself. The addict who comes for help to the system which Doctor Ramirez has organised in the Phoenix Houses is expected, at a later stage in his management,

Introduction

to assist with new addicts coming in for help. The same approach using ex-addicts is followed in the other American programmes known as 'Syanon' and 'Daytop' (Drug Addicts Treated on Probation). One difficulty in Britain is that we do not have as yet enough ex-addicts to go round and form the nucleus of a rehabilitation programme.

What all this means is that the treatment team has to be made up of professionals, lay-people and the addicts themselves if there is to be any real progress. Such a comprehensive approach though ideal in theory is not easy in practice because of the emotional feelings which each of these groups has towards the other two—feelings of rivalry, feelings of sensitivity and feelings of insecurity and threat to status. Quite a lot of time and energy has to be spent working through these difficulties as well as those of the problem itself.

There is one other advantage in using ex-addicts in a rehabilitation programme and that is that they represent living proof that treatment is not impossible. There is a kind of gloomy pessimism current about ever being able to do anything for drug addicts which can well develop into a self-fulfilling prophecy.

It is interesting to ask where this nihilistic attitude comes from. There is a certain realistic basis to it, because programmes of treatment for addicts in a medical setting are notoriously ineffective. As soon as the addict comes out of the treatment situation he tends to return to his drug-taking way of life. But there are irrational components to this pessimistic attitude as well.

Addicts are not easy people to like because it is rarely possible to form that degree of a personal relationship with them which is the traditional basis of much medical and social work. The addict's lack of motivation also works against a traditional helping approach. Saying that

Drugs: the Parents' Dilemma

addicts cannot be helped, or are never cured, can be an expression of our own hostility to the addict and be a covert rejection of his way of life. Some have further suggested that society has a vested interest in keeping the addict as he is in his dependent state, to be a justification and maintenance of the scapegoat function which he so readily fulfils. In other words, the 'goodies' need the 'baddies' to stay as 'baddies': that way the 'goodies' become assured that they still are the 'goodies'.

Having said all this as a way of general background I would now like to turn and look specifically at what parents can do and what society can do in the way of active treatment, rehabilitation and prevention in the future.

14

What Can Parents Do?

TO make this as comprehensive and understandable as possible I will describe what parents can do under two broad headings:

(*a*) What parents can do to prevent their children becoming dependent on drugs.

(*b*) What parents can do once they discover that a young person is taking drugs illicitly.

(*a*) *General Prevention*

Everyone agrees that it is much better and easier to stop a social problem developing, than it is to manage it once established. And with the problem of drugs it is much better and easier to try to prevent young people using drugs than to treat them once they are taking drugs regularly. The first thing parents must do is *to become aware of the danger* and then *to learn how it arises.*

The very purpose of this book and others like it, is to alert parents to the problem and then to suggest how it arises and what steps can be taken to avert it. But what parents read must be informed and based on facts, not fantasy.

The whole subject is too easily bedevilled by myths and legends, especially when it has on occasions been presented in a sensational way in the papers, on the radio and on television. These are the main sources from which

Drugs: the Parents' Dilemma

many parents derive their ideas on controversial issues, so that the media of mass communication have a great responsibility to present accurate and precise information as far as it is available, especially when the information is presented in a semi-authoritative way under the guise of documentary. Factual programmes must be clearly differentiated from works of fiction intended only to be such. Later it will be described how lay-people can form voluntary associations, one of whose aims is the collection of reliable information and its dissemination to members.

Having learned of the danger and what lies behind it, parents must then *keep a sense of proportion*. This is not easy unless they have some good yardstick by which to judge. What must be clearly stated, over and over again is that not all young people who use drugs become dependent upon them, and that using drugs is now in our culture a phase of development for many adolescents.

Statistics like the following are worth repeating—the American experience is that when heroin was freely available one boy in ten tried it, but of these very few became dependent on it. When the drug was freely available before the Harrison Act of 1914, the dependency rate was one in one thousand persons (Laurie). Such experience as we do have in this country so far, would confirm this reduced pattern of usage. Parents should also remember that for all the young people who use barbiturates, amphetamines and cannabis, very few go on to use the hard drugs like heroin, cocaine and methadone.

Next, *parents should set a good example* to their children, by not making flagrant use of drugs of dependency themselves. I am thinking of alcohol, and nicotine and sleeping tablets and tranquillisers. Drinking and smoking should be done in moderation in front of children, and the taking of medically prescribed drugs done discreetly. What is harmful is not so much the taking of these drugs

What Can Parents Do?

(this has to be done for good reasons on many occasions) but a careless attitude towards them; leaving them lying about the house, implying that it does not matter if you take drugs and that no precautions are necessary.

And finally under the general heading of prevention, a most important factor is *the way the children are brought up*.

Psychologists and psychiatrists still disagree with one another, and no doubt will continue to do so, on how to bring up children properly but there are several things known to lead to trouble later. The best way to insure that your children will be disturbed with an increased risk of taking to drugs, and with the chance of becoming dependent upon them, is to do the following:

1. Make them insecure by being inconsistent towards them
2. Make them feel rejected and not wanted
3. Deny them their individuality by treating them as objects
4. Withdraw all love and affection from them or blow hot and cold in an unpredictable way
5. Confuse them about the meaning and values of life
6. Give them no firm guidance on anything by being totally permissive
7. Spoil them by gratifying every whim at once
8. Deny them the opportunity to identify themselves with worthwhile projects in adolescence
9. Take drugs yourself and show them that you do not care if they do the same.

This is not, of course, an exhaustive list but it is what comes to mind. Parents will respond by saying 'Well, we never do things like that do we?' But in fact we do, but not in obvious ways. We do it as parents because we are human and have worries ourselves. The important thing

Drugs: the Parents' Dilemma

again is to be aware of some of the traps and try hard not to fall into them. If we know what is dangerous, we can watch ourselves and reduce the frequency and intensity with which we engage in these activities.

Each of these nine actions carries the implication of the good alternative, but it is all too easy to list them as such, and they become more pious hopes than actual modes of behaviour. That is why I have put them down in this inverse way to make the impact more immediate.

To summarise so far: a young person is more likely to turn to drugs with the risk of becoming dependent upon them if he is brought up in such a way as to feel very insecure, with no personality of his own, an object of his parents' making, if his parents do not set him a good example over the way they use drugs, and if the parents are blind to the risks and how the problem arises.

Eventually, there may come that time when parents are not sure, but believe that one of their adolescents is taking drugs. The *suspicion* may have been there for some time but it is often suppressed because of the implications —lack of trust, uncertainty about the grounds for suspicion, fear of the consequences if the suspicion is proved to be well founded. Many parents report to the doctor that they never knew, that they did not notice anything. And yet, on close questioning there are often signs which might have been noticed at the time but were discounted for the reasons that I have given. It is always easy with hindsight to look back, but even so there are *positive things to look for*.

A very interesting article was published in 1967 by Doctor Rathod and his colleagues from Sussex. They were interested in finding out to what degree addicts and their parents agreed about the signs of being on drugs, particularly of being on heroin. A number of general points were

What Can Parents Do?

made. Firstly, the parents appeared to be poor observers, both for the reasons I have given but also because the addicts do cover up their tracks. Secondly, the parents' powers of observation increased once their vigilance was alerted by the police acting on suspicion. Thirdly, the addicts themselves were good observers, which is not surprising because they are involved very much in the scene and have frequent discussions with their peer group.

The one cardinal sign that brought most of the Sussex addicts to light was jaundice due to dirty syringe technique. This has been used as a possible index in other areas with the same results, so that now a young person who becomes jaundiced is suspected of taking drugs until proven otherwise.

However, there were a number of other signs and these are worth looking at. One of the major difficulties is that the unstable behaviour due to drug taking is very similar to the unstable behaviour that we get in other adolescents who are not taking drugs. In other words, you can get false positives.

In order of judgement of the addicts themselves, these were the signs they recognised when *heroin* is being used:

Small pin-point pupils in the eyes
Fresh injection marks on the arms
Slow slurred speech
Scratching, especially if taken with methedrine or cocaine
Alternating wakefulness and drowsiness
Photophobia—eyes hurt by bright lights
Redness and puffiness of the eyes
Vomiting first thing in the morning
Frequent inspection of the injection sites
Blood spotting on the pyjamas

Drugs: the Parents' Dilemma

Apparatus left lying around—old syringes, needles, teaspoons, matches, etc.

When people are using *cannabis* these are possible signs:

A typical smell like burning weeds
Wide open glazed eyes
Slow slurred speech
Fatuous dreamy look on the face
Tendency to inane laughter
Flushed face and suffused eyes
Relaxed posture and unsteady gait
Lack of interest in what is going on around.

In other words a picture very like the typically intoxicated drunk, apart from a different kind of smell. Cannabis resin is greenish, so cigarettes with greenish tobacco in them are probably reefers.

When people are on *amphetamines* these are possible signs:

Alternating moods of depression and elation
Bright eyed look and lack of social tact
Photophobia, and sometimes crusts round the mouth
Loss of appetite and loss of weight
Sleeping late on Monday mornings
Brittle irritable moods and restlessness
Rapid pulse and flushed face
Staying out all night, especially at weekends.

When people are on *barbiturates* these act as sedatives so that they are drowsy, with slurred speech, and dilated pupils. They can become intoxicated, as with cannabis. When people are on LSD it is very difficult to tell, except when they are 'on a trip' which is characterised by strange dissociated behaviour while they are under the influence

What Can Parents Do?

of hallucinations and other altered perceptions. They tend to take the drug in groups at the weekend so that they can sleep off the late effects of a trip.

There are a number of other *suspicious, but non-specific signs* of drug taking. Lots of unknown visitors coming round for a few minutes (to exchange drugs) or to spend the weekend (a freak out); an increased number of telephone calls especially at weekends (exchanging information about where there may be an interesting party or where drugs can be obtained illicitly—the cafe, the youth club, the market place); a falling off of intellectual performance at school or college for no other reason (due to inability to concentrate and loss of drive); a falling off of personal habits with an assumption of certain fashions in clothes, manner of speech, and length of hair; a cessation of menstruation not due to the obvious cause of pregnancy. The girls will not necessarily show that anything is wrong, but it may slip out in conversation. I should repeat that these signs are non-specific: they can be due to lots of things other than drug taking, but they can arouse suspicions which can be confirmed or refuted by looking for other more positive signs.

(b) Active treatment

If it has been confirmed that drugs are being used illicitly, what can the parents do? I would like to consider this under two headings:

(a) *Persons the parents can contact for help*
(b) *The parent's participation in a management programme.*

Before the parents do turn to someone outside the family, they should stop to consider whether it is really necessary or even desirable. It may be that the drugs are

Drugs: the Parents' Dilemma

being used as part of a passing phase, and to bring in someone from outside may blow this up into something bigger than it really is. It may be seen as a vote of no confidence in the young people by the parents and serve only to drive them further apart from each other. It may kill any attempt at a reconciliation or at least a potentially helpful dialogue between the parents and the adolescent. On the other hand, feelings may be so high on both sides that no meaningful conversation can take place without the aid of a conciliator or an interpreter and it is at this stage that parents should consider to whom they can turn for help.

Whom they will approach first depends on a number of factors, not least of which is availability and willingness to be approached. It will depend also on the setting in which the drug misuse has been discovered—at school or college, at home, by being picked up on suspicion by the police.

The various persons from whom parents could expect some help can be found under four general headings—the educationalists, the medical and social services, the law enforcement agencies and from informed lay organisations.

1. EDUCATIONALISTS

At school, the teacher may be the first to suspect that a pupil is using drugs, usually by observation of behaviour in the classroom or in the playground. He or she will wonder why a promising pupil is doing badly or persistently falling asleep in class or behaving oddly in the company he keeps. The first help a teacher may bring is the disclosure of the problem. The teacher will contact the Headmaster and colleagues and discuss with them the next step. There will always be two considerations here—

What Can Parents Do?

the protection of the other pupils and the care of the person on drugs.

These considerations may act in opposition to each other, in that to protect the others, a Headmaster may have to dismiss a pupil from the school, but this will have a damaging effect on the pupil concerned. What is done will obviously depend on the drugs being used, and whether the pupil is only using them himself or actively trying to give them to other pupils as well. It should be remembered here that the drugs used are more likely to be amphetamines, barbiturates and cannabis. The use of heroin in school is exceptional.

The one advantage which the good teacher has is a relationship with the pupil. If this is built on trust and respect, the teacher may be able to work with the drug user in the early stages after discovery. The teacher can act as an intermediary between the parents and the pupil. Parent Teacher Associations (PTA's) are exploring ways of learning more about the problem and developing channels of communication between the parents and the schools.

The tutor in the university or college of further education is in a similarly well-placed position to help if he knows his students well or is prepared to go some way to do so after drug taking is discovered. At this level the drugs used will be cannabis, LSD, probably amphetamines and possibly heroin and cocaine. The attitude of the university or college, whether it is seen as harshly authoritarian, or prepared to examine the problem further, determine how far the tutor will be able to go in helping a particular student. Again, the important factor is the nature and the degree of the relationship between the helper and the helped.

Educationalists can assist in a more general way and

that is by research into causes, but more particularly into methods of educative propaganda.

A lot has been learned about the different ways of approaching school children and students for health education in general. There have been striking successes, and equally striking failures, with programmes directed against smoking and venereal disease. There is a lot to be learned about audio-visual aids as a tool of propaganda. What makes the best film? How do you expose the dangers, without whetting the appetite for new and forbidden experiences? Are you educating the young on how to use drugs, rather than warning them of the dangers of doing so? How do people of our generation best get across to an audience of teenagers, when the whole debate is based on the generation gap?

These and other questions are fields in which educationalists will be able to offer some help and informed opinion in the future.

2. MEDICAL AND SOCIAL AGENCIES

The first person the family will most likely think of approaching is the general practitioner, especially if they look upon him as the family doctor. Many GP's feel hopelessly inadequate and unprepared when faced with this problem and yet the GP has many vital roles to play whether he is aware of them or not.

(a) He is the medical practitioner of first contact
(b) He is the only doctor who is likely to know the family as a whole
(c) He will probably be the first relatively unemotional arbiter the family will think of turning to
(d) He can act as a lightning conductor, or as the defuser of an emotional time-bomb before it has the chance to explode

What Can Parents Do?

(e) He can determine the degree of dependency on the drug used—is it only a passing phase or has the person become hooked, physically or psychologically?

(f) He can decide whether he himself is going to handle the problem or whether he will ask the help of a specialist colleague

(g) He can support the parents and help them to contain their anxieties, if he can do nothing for the addict

(h) He can try to build up a meaningful relationship with the addict which is a necessary pre-requisite before suggesting he goes for specialist help

(i) He is a prominent member of the containment team which will try to limit the amount of drugs floating free in the community

(j) He can help by protecting the general physical health of the addict, and be on the lookout for weight loss, exhaustion and jaundice.

After a time the GP may decide to refer the addict to the Psychiatric Service, but again before he does so, he should consider what this may mean to the parents and to the addict himself. Addiction is not synonymous with mental illness, although it can in some cases be an expression of it.

All addicts have emotional and personality problems, which either precede the addiction, or certainly develop from it. Being referred to the psychiatrist may induce a resistance which will impede further progress. Many psychiatrists, like the general practitioner, feel unable or unwilling to help with this problem, and those who are willing will often admit that they have as much to learn from the addict as he has from them. Many parents resent

Drugs: the Parents' Dilemma

the implication of mental disorder, but many others are only too willing to 'have something done about it'.

The first person to interview the addict may be the psychiatric social worker rather than the psychiatrist. She has a number of vital roles to play:

(a) She is a mother figure to balance the father figure of the psychiatrist; thus both parental images are presented to the addict

(b) She can be a 'go between' for the family and the clinic, and she can be someone with whom the addict's mother can identify and from whom the mother can get special support

(c) She is in contact with a large number of social agencies who can be approached for help—the Disabled Resettlement Officer (DRO) for employment, the Ministry of Social Security for benefits when the addict is unemployed, help with accommodation problems from the housing authority or sympathetic landladies, guidance from the Children's Department if the addict is under eighteen years of age, from the police and from the probation service. The list is extensive

(d) She can support the psychiatrist by seeing the addict for counselling at times when the psychiatrist may not be available.

The sex of the person offering help can be important because of what happens at home. A boy having difficulties with his father may react adversely to the authority which he may see invested in the psychiatrist. Such a boy will respond better to a female social worker. On the other hand, what may be more important than the actual sex of the helper, is how he is perceived by the addict. An addict may respond to a male doctor because he perceives in him the more feminine attributes of understanding, sympathy, acceptance and sensitivity, and is responding to the maternal function which he projects on to the doctor.

The role of the psychiatrist is a complex one and, as I have already said, is invested with an authority and wisdom which the psychiatrist only wishes he had. Faced with difficult problems, people need to feel that there is someone who has the answers or at least knows where to find them. The psychiatrist has only too readily been cast in this role. This is based on the fact that psychiatrists are asked to help with other addicted persons, such as alcoholics, and are believed to be experts in the addiction field. It is also based on an understanding that addiction arises out of personal conflicts and emotional difficulties which are seen as the province of a psychiatrist.

However, these are assumptions which we have learnt by sorry experience lead to disappointment. Knowledge and experience gained with alcoholics is not necessarily applicable to young heroin users or teenagers using pep pills, and the expertise which the average psychiatrist has built up through his work with adult neurotic and personality disorders likewise does not of itself help him to cope with disturbing adolescents who are acting out their identity problems. Nevertheless, psychiatrists do have a role to play and many have had to learn about the problem of addiction along with the addicts who have been their best teachers. This is the reversal of the traditional role which I have mentioned before.

A psychiatrist does have training in the understanding and analysis of human relationships, and he is able to reveal the emotional factors not only in the addict himself but in the reaction of society to the addict. These skills he brings to this relatively new situation and he is learning how to apply them with benefit to the problem. He works in a number of logically connected steps.

Drugs: the Parents' Dilemma

(a) He begins by assessing the presenting situation—what is to be done and what can be done?
(b) He evaluates the particular personality of the addict: his strengths as well as his weaknesses
(c) He determines the degree of disturbance present: has the young person reached the stage of physical dependence on a hard drug, or is he still at the stage of psychological dependence only? If there is a personality disorder, what chances are there of doing something fairly quickly?
(d) He can select the suitability of the patient for special treatments: should he go into hospital, or can he be treated as an out-patient? Can he be helped by simple support, or will he need more intensive psychotherapy?
(e) He supervises the patient in his subsequent medical and social management, whether it is in the hospital, in a treatment centre or in the community in a hostel
(f) He advises and plays a part as a member of the containment team
(g) Finally, he has an important part to play in public relations work, helping to build up understanding of the problem with members of the general public.

The psychotherapist is a particular kind of psychiatrist. He is specially trained and experienced in giving counselling, which is a kind of informed advice together with helping the addict to see his emotional and relationship problems more clearly. He also gives intensive psychotherapy which is a specialised technique (not the same as psychoanalysis, but derived from it) whereby the addict over a period of time is helped both to gain insight into himself, and to mature so that he can handle relationships better. This form of treatment is not easy to get, it takes

What Can Parents Do?

time, and there are not enough psychotherapists to go round. It has therefore to be rationed for the more disturbed people, and those most likely to be helped by it. The task of the assessing psychiatrist is to make this kind of decision.

In-patient care in hospital can also be selected by the psychiatrist. This is divided into two different phases—the acute stage and the long-term stage. In the *acute stage* an addict may be admitted when:

(a) He is *intoxicated* by drugs or in a *psychotic* state in which he is no longer responsible for himself. The hospital is then acting as a refuge and place of safety where the addict can be detoxicated.

(b) For *assessment* of his need for drugs. Here 'need', by which is meant biological requirements, is to be contrasted with 'want' by which is meant his psychological demands. This is a difficult procedure but it can help to distinguish psychological from physical dependence, and gives a guide as to how much drug a particular patient needs in order to function reasonably well in a community.

(c) For *withdrawal* of his drug. This is the first stage of treatment in which the abstinence syndrome is dealt with either by putting the addict to sleep during a period which would otherwise be very distressing to him or by reducing the drug slowly and replacing it with another drug which the body learns to use instead for example: methadone (physeptone).

In the *long-term stage* which follows, the essential step is the gradual *rehabilitation* of the withdrawn addict so that he learns to give up the drug depending way of life as a solution to his problem, and learns to function in society in a more effective and satisfying way. Hospital experience so far is that the acute stage is fairly easily managed but that most addicts drop out of the long-term stage because of the demands it puts on them through the pressures to return to the drug taking culture which gave them solace before.

Psychiatric hospital care, despite its limitations, does have certain advantages:

(a) The addict comes away out of his family
(b) He comes out of the drug taking group
(c) He is able to have specialist care.

It also has certain disadvantages:

(a) The addict is out of the community where his real problems lie, and where he is ultimately to return
(b) It emphasises the 'badness' and the 'insanity'
(c) It emphasises the rejection of the 'pariah'
(d) It can encourage a sort of 'Lotus Eater' artificial world on the safety of which the addict can in turn become dependent.

Admitting an addict to an ordinary psychiatric hospital ward has repercussions both on the addict and on the other patients. The addict is demanding and difficult by the nature of his disorder; other people resent the time given to him and do not want to mix with him, nor he with them. He can become a scapegoat yet again for the bad things that happen in the hospital—the windows broken, noisy parties, drinking episodes. Special addiction units have been suggested as an answer but money, accommodation and staff in the psychiatric hospitals are all at a premium and spent on other things. Experience so far suggests that apart from the distinct objectives of the acute phase, the management of addicts in the hospital environment will never work anyway, and that alternatives have to be sought.

What Can Parents Do?

The two alternatives being explored at present are the treatment centre (containment unit) and the hostel.

(a) The treatment centre

These have been set up as required since the changes in the Law in relationship to drug addiction as described in Part One. Most of them are in London, but also in the bigger provincial cities where there is a growing addict population.

These centres have two functions. The first function is to *contain* the amount of free drugs available in the community and essentially this means heroin, cocaine, methadone and methedrine. The philosophy of a containment policy will be discussed in detail later.

The second function is to provide a means of *regular supervision and prescription* for the registered addicts on an out-patient basis. The addict attends weekly or twice weekly and is seen by his doctor who tries to build up a meaningful relationship with him. Prescriptions are made out for each day, but are sent direct to the local chemist from whom the addict has to collect his daily supply. This is to prevent forgery of prescriptions and handing out of drugs to others.

Most of these centres have only been functioning since April 1968 so it is early yet to say how effective they are, but at the time of writing it would appear that the containment aspect is beginning to work. This is based on the observation that the amount of free heroin available in London is now much less and what is available is costing very much more on the black market.

(b) The Addict Hostel

These have yet to be set up in this country in a general way but the justification for them is based on the most effective programmes of care in America. Three organisations

—Syanon, Daytop and Phoenix Houses—depend on the ex-addict as the most effective member of the treatment team. They are also based on the philosophy that the only person who can help an addict is the addict himself, and that he has to learn this truth for himself.

The hostel is in the community where the addict lives—it is a part of his normal world, not like the hospital. He can walk in and refer himself for treatment. Whether he stays or goes is very much up to him and the other addicts. These other addicts will soon expose all his weak arguments like 'I can't help it' or 'this is bigger than me' or 'I will never be able to do without drugs'.

There is a graded programme whereby the addict gradually learns to assume more and more responsibility for himself and then for the other addicts. The final stage is reached when the graduate ex-addict is helping in the induction of new 'walk-ins'. The work of Doctor Ramirez in New York shows that the whole Phoenix programme may take up to three years—it is no quick answer: learning is slow and painful but more likely to be maintained. Doctor Ramirez claims that only seven out of his first 124 addicts treated went back on to heroin three and a half years later, a relapse rate which compares very favourably with many other treatment programmes.

But there are difficulties here. Neighbourhoods are understandably not keen to have a drug addict hostel in them. Property is at a premium in big cities and where is the money to come from? Given premises, who is to be responsible for them? Who is going to supervise the addicts? And so on. Despite the difficulties, which are there to be overcome, this approach may well be the most fruitful for the future, but applies more to the person addicted to hard drugs than to the soft ones.

The role of the *police and probation service* has been described by Superintendent Jones in Part Two and the

What Can Parents Do?

role of the *lay person* is described later in this book by Doctor Myers of Cambridge.

These then are some of the people and facilities that parents can turn to for help, but asking for help and getting it to some extent does not absolve the parents from a continuing involvement in what is happening.

I have suggested that the relationship of the drug user to his parents plays an important part in the genesis of this problem, so that this relationship must be kept under observation while the treatment of the drug user is being pursued.

Parents will want to keep in touch with teachers and headmasters through PTAs and direct contact. They will need help and advice for their own emotional problems from the family doctor. They will want to keep in contact with a psychiatric social worker and the probation officer. They will want to see the psychiatrist and he will want to hear from them. But in all these contacts it must be remembered that a relationship is being considered, and the helping agencies must be seen as an agent of the relationship and never seen as the unilateral agent of one side against the other. Each side must feel free to contact the helpers and be helped by them but never in a possessive exclusive way which denies the need for access and for help to the other.

What Can the Community Do?

So far, I have been looking at the reactions of parents and what they can do as individuals faced with this problem, or what they can try to do to prevent it from arising. But parents and those to whom they turn for help—teachers, doctors, social workers, psychologists, and other involved non-professionals like themselves, are all members of our society. In a real sense, we can ask what the community can do, the community of all those in society concerned on a personal basis, or in a general way with this problem.

I have described already how this is a problem for society; a problem it helps to create, a problem which is confronting it, and a problem it cannot run away from but on which it must make up its mind where it stands, and what it is prepared to do about it. Doctor Kenneth Myers, a colleague who has worked in the community with parents and other lay people, now describes what he believes the community can and ought to do.

WHAT THE COMMUNITY CAN DO

(Dr. Kenneth Myers, Chairman, Cambridge Association for Prevention of Drug Addiction)

Drug dependence has been called a community mental health problem; it would therefore seem reasonable to expect that the community as a whole, not just professionally involved groups, could and should contribute to a

What Can the Community Do?

policy of prevention, containment and treatment of the problem. But how can lay people, ordinary concerned citizens, provide solutions when those with relevant skills have shown a conspicuous lack of success over the years, in this country and elsewhere?

How is the ordinary citizen to know where to direct his energies when there are social problems enough which are nowhere near solution: those of the aged, the homeless, and of alcoholics to mention a few underprivileged groups in our society. But, as we have seen, it is the rapidity of the spread of drug abuse particularly amongst young people, that concentrates our efforts on finding the answers to this particular problem.

Before we can deal rationally and effectively with drug misuse, certain changes must come about, at national and local level. Some are already happening. A lot of work is needed before others are initiated.

Changes at national level involve, of course, changes in the law. How freely available are drugs of dependence going to be? What is the effectiveness, desirability or even relevance of, for example, the law making cannabis a prohibited substance when that law is, to a large extent, unenforceable? Do we need changes here? If so, of what kind? Do we make it available on prescription, tax it heavily, or just modify the penalties for possessing it? The appropriate answer depends on what effects cannabis has as a drug when used in a variety of social settings. We have little knowledge to help us find answers. The need for research is painfully obvious.

One might quote the virtual proscription of the amphetamines in Japan since the mid-1950s as another example of change at national level. Do we follow suit? Do we, as concerned people, challenge the doctors to show cause why the amphetamines should *not* be prohibited?

Other changes in the law, already enacted, are referred to in a previous section. But the law affects us all, and we should, therefore, have some say in framing it, provided that our contribution is on an informed basis. It is almost impossible for the individual lay person to bring much pressure to bear on the central legislators, but an organised, properly constituted body can. It can act as a pressure group; it can collect, collate and disseminate information in a variety of ways; it can initiate research, establish centres for treatment and rehabilitation under medical supervision; it can provide support for those needing it, for parents of drug users, and others in touch with them: teachers, youth leaders, doctors.

A national organisation does exist whose aims are almost precisely those outlined above. The Association for the Prevention of Addiction* was formed early in 1967 following the publication in the *Guardian* of an article entitled 'My Son takes Heroin'. It described the reaction of a mother to the discovery that her son used the drug. It was a brilliantly written article which suggested the formation of an association to tackle drug problems, and it evoked an immediate response from hundreds of people scattered all over the country.

The Association now has central London offices, a full-time organiser and branches in most big towns. It is a registered Charity. It gave invaluable help during what has come to be known as the Soho drugs crisis of 1968, when one doctor, who was supplying many youngsters with prescriptions for heroin, had to stop prescribing dangerous drugs. There is an Education Committee which has formulated a policy for disseminating information in schools and colleges, and the Association is advised by prominent professionals in the field of drug dependence.

It is at local level, perhaps, that the most immediately

* A.P.A., 16 King Street, London, W.C.2.

What Can the Community Do?

fruitful changes can occur. Groups of people can meet to express opinions, explore social implications, find facts of local significance, spread knowledge, apply pressure, provide facilities and generally make themselves felt.

From the outset they will meet the difficulties facing voluntary workers entering a professional field: the professionals find it hard to accept the volunteers, and the volunteers feel that the professionals are not moving quickly enough. It is even worse in the field of drug dependence where the boundaries of responsibility are not clear and there is not yet enough knowledge to make them clearer. But any organisation attempting to work in this field must get itself accepted by professional bodies.

Co-operation between medical, social work and lay organisations is the cornerstone of any coherent policy for coping with drug problems. Just as recent legislation has envisaged co-operation between police, chemists and treatment centres as the foundation on which any policy of containment is built, so co-operation between these and other organisations is the foundation for *helping* those with drug problems.

Perhaps some of the activities that can be undertaken by local groups can be illustrated by our experience in Cambridge.

The Cambridge Association for the Prevention of Drug Addiction was formed in June 1967, to bring together those affected by and those concerned by the problems of drug dependence; to disseminate reliable information about drug dependence; to stimulate research into, and where necessary to press for facilities for treatment of drug dependence. Those playing a leading role in getting people together were, for the most part, mothers of adolescent children, teachers and lecturers. Later, general

Drugs: the Parents' Dilemma

practitioners, a psychiatrist, and a probation officer were involved.

All of these people, the doctors included, had little knowledge of the abuse of drugs. The first step was to arrange a series of public meetings to be addressed by those with knowledge of the subject. At one meeting, three heroin users made it clear that they had received little help from the ordinary medical and psychiatric facilities provided in the area. Something more was needed, if only a place where they could meet, they said, to talk about their problems. Out of this complaint arose a regular, once-weekly meeting of drug users and helpers which, at the time of writing, continues, and which has been described in the medical journals.* (*Lancet*, 1968.)

At these meetings, a number of drug users which varies from one or two to ten or twelve, meets an average of seven or eight helpers. The meetings are completely informal. Discussion ranges widely, but usually centres round the problems of work and the attitudes of family and society. When police activity increases, the resulting anxiety is freely expressed in the group, sometimes in a rather paranoid way. Changes in local policy and in clinic arrangements were discussed. Specific requests for help—for work, for emergency overnight lodgings, for intercession with their own doctor—are thrashed out and often acted on.

The parents of drug users, too, have their problems, not least of which are feelings of guilt, anger and bewilderment. It soon became apparent that, while some sort of help had become available for drug users themselves, their parents had no such support. Efforts were made to contact them, and two groups of parents now meet at monthly intervals. Some of the difficulties of communication between parents and drug users can be eased. Some

---

* *Lancet*, i, 805–6, 1968.

What Can the Community Do?

of the frustrations, criticisms, hopes and desires each side feels about the other can be aired with a little of the heat and hurtfulness removed.

The Association quickly learned to disseminate information, by providing, on request, copies of the growing volume of literature, by continuing its series of public meetings, and by giving talks to other bodies. Because this group of voluntary workers now has first-hand knowledge of the problems of drug users, and has coped with a variety of emergency situations, it has been asked to provide speakers to a wide range of organisations, from professional bodies to church gatherings, to schools and parent-teacher associations.

The Association very early on realised that there would be little point in pressing for facilities for treatment of drug dependence unless some idea of the size of the local problem was obtained. A start was made when the psychiatrist in the organisation asked local general practitioners to indicate the numbers of heroin users known to them, since, of all drugs, heroin at that time was likely to be the one whose use could most accurately be measured. The help of a professional research team from London was invoked, with the full knowledge and consent of the local medical authorities, and an accurate assessment of heroin use in the town was made. Research into the progress of those contacted continues.

Another function that the Association fulfils is that of indicating courses of action for the future, and of suggesting ideas for discussion. It is entitled to do this because of its first-hand knowledge of the people whose needs are being met. It has been apparent that many of the Cambridge drug users—heroin users in particular—have formed an in-group, tending to become divorced from society, adrift from normal activity. The essentially lay active membership of the Association has been able to forge a link with the community so that the group is not entirely out of touch.

It follows from this that they have been able to suggest that future thinking on treatment and rehabilitation of drug users should indicate that it would best be carried out, not in a hospital setting, with its emphasis on beds and sickness, where the significant problems of parental-type authority would loom very large, and where the problems of dependence and rehabilitation back to the community are accentuated, but in a community setting.

The users themselves would be active, responsible members of a smaller community, using and developing the personality resources they have rather than emphasising their dependence on drugs. They would be in touch with the ordinary world, and, essentially, the idea would be to replace the support given by drugs with the support given by a community in which they themselves have a big stake. The idea is *not* new—communities have existed for centuries, as in monasteries and places of retreat; they are found in the fields of education and mental health. The concept is used in the United States in the treatment of drug dependence.

So much, then, for the exciting, wearing and, at times, discouraging business of involvement in local problems of drug dependence.

It is necessary, at all times, to be aware that the fullest communication and co-operation is necessary amongst those attempting even supportive work. It is very easy to become deeply involved in one particular problem to the exclusion of all others. It is necessary to remember that there are very few psychiatrists, for example, committed full-time to drug problems, and that what may seem tardiness in responding immediately to a call for help is probably, in fact, a realistic response to one call out of very many commitments.

What Can the Community Do?

The problem for the lay person is as much when *not* to, as *when* to help. It is essential that he seldom acts alone. It is very desirable that he has professional advice available. It is mandatory that somebody else knows what he is doing. An Association is in a good position to provide him with the necessary background.

There remain two big questions facing our community with regard to the problem of illicit drug use. The first concerns the advisability and the effectiveness of compulsory treatment for drug dependent persons, and the second concerns a philosophy and policy of containment.

(a) Compulsory Treatment

The argument for compulsory treatment is based on the premise that drug dependent individuals, by virtue of their personality disorder and the effects on them of taking drugs, cannot decide or choose for themselves whether they need treatment or not, and so the community should decide for them in their own best interest as well as that of society. This means in effect depriving individuals of their freedom and compulsorily detaining them for treatment.

There is, of course, a precedent already in law for taking such action in the Mental Health Act 1959 by which persons believed to be suffering from such a degree of mental disorder that they cannot make a valid decision about themselves can be compulsorily placed into a psychiatric hospital for treatment. Compulsory treatment also assumes that addicts thus treated do better than if they are not treated, but the evidence for this assumption has to be carefully examined.

Drugs: the Parents' Dilemma

What society does with its addicts will depend on the attitude society has towards them. There are three basic attitudes at the present time, not necessarily exclusive of each other.

1. *That addiction is an illness*

This is the position of the Brain Committee, and the logical next step is to treat the illness, again always assuming that it is susceptible to treatment.

2. *That addiction is a crime*

This is the position of those who see the illicit use of drugs contravening the existing drug laws, and the logical next step is to punish the offenders.

3. *That addiction is an undesirable social habit*

This is the position of the establishment, which sees the habit as dangerous both to the addict and to society. The next logical step is to attempt to eradicate it.

All these attitudes can be rationalised to support the argument for compulsory detention.

1. *Treatment of the illness*

The Mental Health Act can be used to compel an addict into a psychiatric hospital for treatment. *Section 29* can be used when there is an emergency and the addict is so psychologically disturbed by virtue of the effects of the drugs he has taken, that he is a danger to himself or to others, and is unable to make a valid decision about treatment for himself. Such a section operates only for seventy-two hours. *Section 25* allows compulsory admission if there are grounds to suspect that the addict is suffering from such a degree of mental disorder that he requires observation and treatment. The section operates for up to twenty-eight days. *Section 26* allows for compulsory treatment if the addict is suffering from mental illness, severe sub-normality or psychopathic disorder (but only if under twenty-one years of age). This section operates for one year in the first instance and can be extended. Persons detained under this section have the right of appeal to Mental Health Review Tribunals. The Mental Health Act, however, stresses that the person who is detained must be suffering from mental disorder, and in *Section 4 (5)* it expressly excludes promiscuity or immoral conduct as grounds for detention under this heading.

Apart from the issues of compulsory admission, I have already indicated that there are limitations to what treatment in a hospital can achieve, and these apply whether the patient is compulsorily detained or not. The addict's full co-operation is paramount, and this is all the less likely to be achieved if he is detained in hospital against his will.

2. *Punishment of the offender*

An addict may be fined, imprisoned or put on probation, and in any combination of all three, the severity of the sentence depending on the offence and whether he has been pushing the drugs as well as using them. The penal approach may be used to punish, but also to rehabilitate.

However, if an addict is sent to prison in order to receive treatment, he should be sent to a prison which specialises in this work. So far in Britain such facilities are difficult to get—the institutions are overcrowded, they lack trained and experienced staff, and the addict runs the risk of being picked up by recidivists and persuaded to join a Black Market organisation once he gets outside.

In America there are two Public Health Service prison hospitals, at Lexington, Kentucky and at Fort Worth,

Texas. Research with a twelve year follow-up on one hundred addicts discharged from the Federal Hospital at Lexington, showed one year abstinence rates (not using drugs for one year after discharge) for the following treatment regimes:

Hospitalisation alone: 4 per cent
Short-term imprisonment (less than nine months): 4 per cent
Long-term imprisonment (more than nine months): 13 per cent
Imprisonment plus subsequent parole: 67 per cent

This work suggests that probation backed up with an effective threat of re-imprisonment does offer better long-term results. This outcome is confirmed in other studies; for example, 34 per cent of men on probation in the Californian Civil Commitment Programme have not taken drugs for one year. Experienced workers in the United States feel that an element of coercion is necessary but such programmes face a dilemma: repressive legislation has been shown to be ineffective (for example after the Harrison Act of 1914), but the threat of imprisonment does increase the chances of helping an addict on probation.

It is still debatable as to how much the experience of workers in addiction in America can be transferred and applied to addiction in Britain. Programmes cannot be lifted wholesale and transplanted, but general trends and response patterns can be observed.

3. *Suppression of an undesirable habit*

From the viewpoint of society, the community wishes its sick members to be treated, and its offending members to be punished. Society is concerned with the care of its individual deviant members, but it is also concerned with limiting the spread of an undesirable 'contagion' to other 'wholesome' members. The analogy of the spread and control of an epidemic has already been used. Basically, society is concerned with containment as well as with treatment.

(b) A Containment Policy

A containment policy has two main objectives:

1. To restrict the availability of free-floating drugs in the community and thus to minimise the creation of newly-addicted persons
2. To gain some measure of control over the management of existing identified addicts.

The setting up of a containment programme involves a number of steps.

1. The identification of cases. The recognition of individual addicts has already been described, but these methods can also be applied to whole communities; for example, an examination of all recent cases of infectious jaundice in young people brought to light an unsuspected number who were injecting themselves with heroin in a New Town.

2. The establishment of central recording systems. These should operate both nationally as in the Home Office Register and locally so that the identified cases can be known, management policies determined, and changes in trends notified.

3. Opening up channels of communication between all interested parties—doctors, nurses, social workers, police, probation officers, teachers, headmasters, parents and

Drugs: the Parents' Dilemma

addicts themselves. This is both to disseminate what hard information is available, but also to try to break down traditional attitudes and prejudices.

4. Regular co-ordination meetings of all those involved in the containment, to maintain up-to-date information (briefing function) but also to go some way to breaking down the emotional barriers and resistances between helpers which have already been described.

5. The establishment of a general policy and attitude to the problem at national and local levels. This means determining what goals are being aimed for, and what sanctions are going to be used against those who infringe the containment policy. Here there is a basic dilemma, and not easily resolved, between being too inflexible, rigid, harshly authoritarian on the one hand, and being too permissive and easily manipulated on the other. It will be recalled that this is the very dilemma facing a parent. The community acts as a parent towards all the addicts for whom it is responsible.

6. Setting up basic treatment facilities as already described—hospital units, out-patient clinics, treatment centres, hostels, lay organisations, etc.

7. Organising a systematic method of continuing public education, so that the community should know what the current problems are and what is being done to try to come to terms with them.

A local containment programme may decide not to make any drugs available at all. This is a heroic stand, but there can be two dangers:

(a) Reinforcing the setting up of a local Black Market in drugs
(b) Driving drug dependent persons into other areas of the country where drugs are easier to come by.

What Can the Community Do?

On the other hand the containment programme may decide to make drugs available to certain individuals but under strict control. This means the setting up of a *containment clinic*, which is based on the assumption that drug dependent persons will be driven to get hold of drugs anyway, and that it is better to provide them in the first instance under control. This may help to develop a relationship with the addicted person which can later be used in persuading them to give up the use of drugs in favour of other ways of dealing with their stresses.

Such a containment clinic will prescribe those drugs on which the addicts are physically dependent. Other less dangerous drugs will be given to replace those on which addicts are psychologically dependent. There is high security over prescriptions which are only made available to those who have been assessed as being in need of them. Only that amount which the addict needs will be given to prevent as far as possible stock-piling in the community.

Such clinics are still in the experimental stage and reveal the strong emotional forces at work between the addicts and those trying to help. The addicts continue to test the limits by refusing to come, turning up late, sending others to pick up their supplies, trying to borrow one day's supply against another, always trying to get more from the doctor or from the chemist. In other words making endless demands for immediate gratification.

The staff, in turn, feel that there is a constant battle to be consistent, not to be permissive nor to be conned into giving more drugs than is necessary, but at the same time not to be aggressive and authoritarian in the face of the relentless pressure for more.

Constant review of the situation will be necessary to know whether a containment programme has been effective or not. Paradoxically, a containment policy is

Drugs: the Parents' Dilemma

THE FIELD OF OPERATIONS

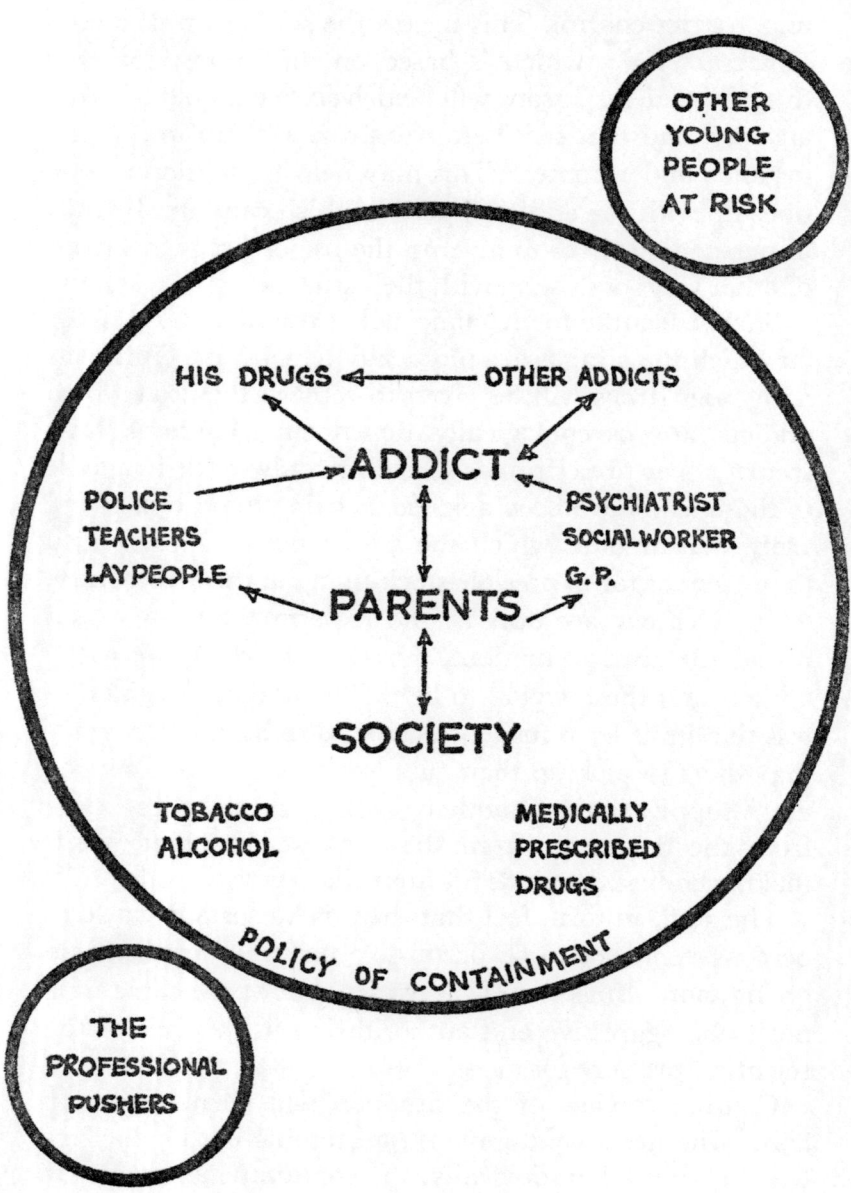

What Can the Community Do?

designed to get rid of the Black Market, and yet the rising costs of illicit drugs with risk of professional pushers taking over for profit, may be the first indication that containment is working.

Figure Two (p. 144) outlines the field of operations of a containment policy.

16

A Final Perspective on Drug Use

AT this stage, it is helpful to look back over what has been discussed, to try to get drug taking into a proper perspective.

At the outset I said that one of the greatest emotional stumbling blocks in this field is the mythology about what drug taking entails. All the propaganda has naturally enough emphasised the bad things and the dangers of taking drugs. This is necessary in a campaign designed to prevent people indulging in a habit which is believed to be socially undesirable, but it is harmful to stress the bad and the negative side of drug taking and to forget that there is a good side.

As we go on and gain more experience and insight into why people take drugs and what happens to them when they do, we discover that the situation and outcome is not as gloomy as once was thought. Also we learn that it is as wrong to class everyone who uses drugs under the general title of 'drug addict' as it is to assume that all drugs act in the same way and are equally dangerous. Each individual has to be studied separately and each pattern of drug use evaluated on its own.

I believe that there are a number of *good things to say to parents* about drugs:

1. Many young people who are in contact with drug users do not go on to use drugs themselves.

A Final Perspective on Drug Use

2. For such young people there may be an initial period of experimentation, a flirtation with drugs, but the affair does not last long.

3. For those who do go and use drugs regularly, it is often a stage in psychological development, arising out of the emotional needs of the time. It is a phase which, having served these needs, is left behind with no ill effects.

4. Those young people who begin by using soft drugs like the barbiturates and the pep pills, rarely go on to hard drugs like heroin and cocaine. Those who do, are usually more psychologically disturbed and would have graduated to the use of heroin anyway.

5. Even if young people do use hard drugs like heroin and cocaine, theirs is not an inevitable road to degradation and entry into membership of a drifting criminal sub-culture. For some this does happen but it is not inevitable for all.

6. Certain young people 'mature' on the use of heroin. Provided it is obtained regularly and in clean supplies, these people are often better in that they can work and cope with their problems. They can also mature *out* of the habit after a time. Using heroin is a way of going into 'cold storage' until they are ready to cope, but the method has its dangers.

7. It is believed that taking drugs may protect certain predisposed young people from breakdown into serious mental illness. Many of the backgrounds and root causes are similar. It is as though working at being an addict provides an identity without which the young person could slide into a psychosis of the schizophrenic type. Here the choice lies between taking drugs for a number of years with all the known dangers, or having to go into a psychiatric hospital with the risk of becoming a long-term psychiatric patient.

What of the future?

Drugs: the Parents' Dilemma

No one really knows. I have tried to outline what is known up to the present time, but the scene is always changing. What we know today may be inappropriate tomorrow. We still have a great deal to learn about drug taking.

The important thing is to be able to provide facilities whereby people can get help who need it, and create an atmosphere which allows learning to take place, and does not smother it beneath over-rigorous legislation or beneath the heat of emotional rejection.

Questions Parents Ask

This is a collection of the main questions I have been asked by parents when I have talked with them individually, talked to them in a group or talked with them at meetings of Parent Teacher Associations.

The questions which parents ask are the kind of questions which teachers ask as well.

They are the kind of questions which the community has to ask and to find answers to, if there is going to be an effective programme of treatment and containment. The places in this book where an answer has been attempted are indicated in brackets after the question and can be identified from the Contents on Page 5.

Which drugs are dangerous? (Chapter 5)
What is meant by hard drugs and soft drugs? (Chapter 4)
Are the soft drugs less dangerous? (Chapter 4)
Why do young people take drugs? (Chapter 8)
Are all young people at risk? (Chapter 12)
What kind of people take drugs? (Chapter 12)
What happens to people when they take drugs?
(Chapter 6)
Is the problem growing in size? (Chapter 6)
How do you know if someone is on drugs? (Chapter 14)
What can a parent do to prevent children taking drugs?
(Chapter 14)
What can be done about drug taking? (Part 3)

Drugs: the Parents' Dilemma

Who can a parent or teacher turn to for help?
(Chapter 14)
What part do the police play in the drug problem?
(Chapter 10)
Is compulsory treatment effective? (Chapter 15)
What does addiction mean? (Chapter 1)
What causes people to become addicted? (Chapter 5)
Can anyone become addicted? (Chapter 5)
Why do so many people use drugs today? (Chapter 11)
Is cannabis smoking safe? (Chapter 12)
Do people go on to hard drugs after soft drugs?
(Chapter 12)
Are there different types of drug addict? (Chapter 12)
How do the different drugs work? (Chapter 5)
Where do addicts get their drugs from? (Chapter 12)
What are the penalties for taking drugs? (Chapter 7)

Drug Taking Slang

Slang is a jargon language used by an in-group to identify its members and to make others feel excluded. It is a means of demonstrating a particular way of life. Slang, to be a living language has to change and grow, so that the vocabulary is variable, but some basic words and phrases remain throughout the vicissitudes of fashion.

Here are some of the more basic words used by young people who are taking drugs:

DRUGS

JUNK, H, HORSE, STUFF   heroin, hence Junkie
COKE, C, SNOW   cocaine
SUGAR, ACID, INSTANT ZEN   LSD
HASH, POT, SMOKE   cannabis
RESIN   cannabis resin (hashish)
REEFER   cigarette doped with cannabis
SPLIFF   another word for reefer
PEP, BLUES, BLACK BOMBERS, BENNIES, DEX, SWEETS   amphetamines
GOOF BALLS, SLEEPERS   barbiturates
METH   methedrine
SNIFFERS   things which are volatile and inhaled
SPEEDBALL   a mixture of heroin and cocaine which is injected

Drugs: the Parents' Dilemma

JACK   one tablet of heroin which is equal to one-sixth of a grain (ten milligrammes) of heroin
DOPE   general word for drugs

EFFECTS OF DRUGS

STONED   intoxicated by cannabis, hence 'stoned out of his mind'
FLIPPED   like 'stoned'
BUZZ, FLASH   effect of injecting heroin
COME DOWN   the effect of exhilaration wearing off
HOOKED   dependent on drugs
HUNG UP   unable to get drugs, depressed
COLD TURKEY   sudden uncovered withdrawal of a drug (abstinence syndromes)
DROP OUT   abdicate out of society
FREAK OUT   effect of LSD, a trip

DRUG ACTIVITIES

SCORING   borrowing or buying drugs illicitly
PUSHING   peddling drugs to others
TURNING ON   persuading someone else to use drugs
SCRATCHING   on the look out for drugs
MAKE   to obtain drugs
KICKING   giving up drugs, hence 'kicking the habit'
CUT   adulterated (drugs)
CLEAN   not on drugs

METHODS OF USING DRUGS

SKIN POPPING   subcutaneous injection
SHOOT, MAINLINE   to inject into a vein, hence 'shooting junk'
FIX   injection of a narcotic
GOOF   spoil a fix
TRIP   taking LSD, hence 'going on a trip'

Drug Taking Slang

CHIPPING   only using heroin at weekends or in small irregular amounts

DRUG APPARATUS

BUSINESS   apparatus for injecting drugs
GEAR   belongings, including drugs, syringe, etc.
SCRIPT   legal prescription for drugs
AMP   ampoule
GUN   needle
MACHINE   syringe

PEOPLE INVOLVED

CONNECTION   person from whom drugs are obtained
SCENE   drug taking sub-culture
FUZZ   police
UNCLE   an informer

PLACES

PAD   room of the drug taker
SHOOTING GALLERY   place where drugs are regularly injected such as a waiting room or public convenience

Some Useful Addresses

The Association for the Prevention of Addiction (A.P.A.), 16 King Street, London, W.C.2.
Association of Parents of Addicts, c/o The Association for the Prevention of Addiction.
The Chelsea Addiction and Research Centre, 88 Beaufort Street, London, S.W.3.
The Research Unit for Drug Addiction, Maudsley Hospital, London.
Spelthorne St. Mary, Thorpe, Egham, Surrey.
The Chief Inspector, The Home Office Drugs Branch, Romney House, Marsham Street, London, S.W.1.
The National Association for Mental Health (N.A.M.H.), 39 Queen Anne Street, London, W.1.
The National Association of Probation Officers (N.A.P.O.), 6 Endsleigh Street, London, W.C.1.
The Department of Health and Social Security, Alexander Fleming House, Elephant and Castle, London, S.E.1.

Further Reading

Drugs and the Police, Terence Jones (Butterworths).
Social Problems of Drug Abuse, Frank Dawtry (Probation Special).
Drugs, Peter Laurie (Penguin Special S249).
The Reports of the Brain Committee (HMSO 1961, 1965).
Drug Dependence, Antony Wood (The Bristol Council for Social Service).
Drugs and Civil Liberties, The National Council for Civil Liberties.
Drugs and Young People, Sister Patricia (Riverside Press).
Drugs: Probe No. 2, Christian Education Movement (June 1967).
Drugs for Young People: Their Use and Misuse (Religious Educational Press).
Drug Addiction, The Office of Health Economics No. 25.
The Tunnel Back (Syanon), L. Yablonsky. Deals with Rehabilitation in the USA.
Drugs: Connexions Series (Penguin Books).
Various pamphlets by the Association for Prevention of Addiction.

Index

abstinence syndrome 20, 32, 39, 41, 125
Addict Hostel 127
Addiction Services Agency, N.Y. 108
alcohol 7, 8, 14, 15, 29, 35, 36, 39, 45, 51, 71, 79, 112
amphetamines 8, 11, 13, 28, 29, 35, 38, 40, 42, 48, 52, 57, 79, 80, 95, 99, 102, 112, 116, 119
amylobarbitone 35, 38
analgesics 29
aspirin 7, 25–7
Association for the Prevention of Addiction 132

barbiturates 7, 13, 28, 29, 35, 36, 38, 40, 48, 52, 95, 100–2, 112, 116, 119, 147
Bewley, Dr. Thomas 51, 54
Brain Committee, 19, 56, 58, 138
butobarbitone 35

caffeine 7, 25, 27
Californian Civil Commitment Programme 140
Cambridge Association for Prevention of Drug Addiction 130, 133
cannabis 8, 11, 14, 28, 30, 35, 43, 44, 48, 52, 53, 56, 58, 59, 79, 81, 93, 100, 102, 112, 116, 119, 131
Children's Department 122
cocaine 29, 32, 35, 42, 49, 52, 53, 56–8, 81, 100, 102, 112, 115, 119, 147
codeine 7, 27, 29, 40
containment clinics 143

Dangerous Drugs Act 1965 13, 45, 56, 58
Dangerous Drugs Act 1967 20, 56, 58
Dangerous Drugs (Notification Addicts) Regulations 58
Dangerous Drugs (Prevention of Misuse) Act 1964 39, 47, 59, 57
Dangerous Drugs (Supply of Addicts) Regulations 58
Daytop 109, 128
Dexamphetamine 38
Dexedeine 38
dextroamphetamine 38
dimethyltriptamine 47
Disabled Resettlement Officer (DRO) 122
D.M.T. 58
Doors of Perception, The 47
Drinamyl 38
Durophet 38

Erdo-carditis 55

Federal Bureau of Narcotics 54
Federal Hospital, Lexington 139, 140
Federal Hospital, Fort Worth 139

general practitioner 120, 121, 134
Geneva Convention 1925 56

hallucinogens 26, 30, 35, 45, 46, 68, 79, 86
Harrison Act 1914 112, 140
hepatitis 55, 101

heroin 8, 12, 26, 29, 31–4, 40–3, 49, 51–4, 57–9, 78–81, 93, 100, 102, 112, 115, 119, 135, 141, 147
Home Office 48, 51, 54
Home Office register 49, 141
Huxley, Aldous 47
hypnotics 29

Inter-Departmental Committee on Drug Addiction 19, 56, 58

Jaundice 101, 115, 141
Jones, Chief-Superintendent 77–84, 128

Laurie 112
Leary, Timothy 47
Librium 15
L.S.D. 8, 13, 14, 26, 28, 30, 33, 45, 46, 53, 58, 79, 81, 90, 100, 102, 116, 119

Mandrax 15
Marihuana 44
Mental Health Act 1959 137–9
Mental Health Review Tribunals 139
mescaline 8, 25, 30, 47, 58
Methadone 12, 29, 40, 112, 125
methedrine 11, 29, 38, 39, 58, 59, 81, 100, 102, 115
Ministry of Social Security 122
Misuse of Drugs Act 1971 12
morphine 24, 29, 40
Myers, Dr. K. 16, 129, 130

nicotine 7, 25, 27, 35, 112

ololinqui 26
opiates 12, 14, 31, 35, 40, 48, 54–6
opium 24, 26, 40, 42

Pentothal 38
pethidine 29, 40
Pharmacy and Poisons Act 1933 36, 57
phenobarbitone 35
Phoenix Houses 108, 128
physeptone 12, 29, 40, 100, 102, 125
psilocybin 25, 47
Psychedelia 47, 86
psychiatric service 121, 122, 138
psychiatrist 122–5, 129, 134–6
psychotherapist 124, 125

quinalbarbitone 35

Ramirez, Dr. 108, 128
Rathod, Dr. 114

Sandoz 45
sedatives 29, 86
sepsis 54, 55
stimulants 29, 86
S.T.P. 47
Syanon 109, 128

therapeutic addicts 49, 51
tranquillisers 7, 28, 29, 112
Treatment Centre 12, 57, 127, 133, 142
Tuinal 35

Valium 15, 29

W.H.O. 20
Winick, C. 20
withdrawal effects 20, 32, 34, 36, 39, 41, 43, 45, 47
Wootton Committee 11